The People of Many Names

'This is a book for those more or less new to the story of the Jewish people. The facts are told with a conciseness and freshness that will appeal to many who have not yet been able to read widely on the subjects covered.

Steve Maltz writes, unashamedly, as a Jewish believer in Jesus and for this reason is able to bring some very challenging insights into history both past and present. His closing chapter is a must-read for all who are concerned with the blessing of the church and of the world, and provides an intelligent call to prayer for the Jewish people and to involvement in the present battle over Israel.'

Derek White, founder of Christian Friends of Israel

'Steve Maltz looks at the life and history of the Jewish people. Starting at the very beginning and sweeping through to recent events, Steve gives a fast-paced and witty, but both insightful and perceptive framework for his readers to gain a meaningful overview of the Jewish people and their relationship with God and the Nations. Maybe this second book should have been subtitled, 'everything you wanted to know about the Jewish people but were afraid to ask'!

Particularly helpful is the way that the author delineates the Jewish people as a nation over Jewish individuals in their relationship with God and their destiny. This is an excellent book for those who are curious as it provides an introduction for those seeking further study.'

Fred Wright, author and Director of Chesed.

'I think it's brilliant – inspired – a great read – of interest to both Jews and Christians – a breath of fresh air – and timely! What more can I say!'

Julia Fisher, writer and broadcaster

The People of Many Names

Towards a Clearer Understanding of the Miracle of the Jewish People

Steve Maltz

Authentic

09 08 07 06 05   7 6 5 4 3 2 1

First published 2005 by Authentic Media,
9 Holdom Avenue, Bletchley, Milton Keynes, Bucks,
MK1 1QR, UK and
129 Mabilization Drive, Waynesboro,
GA 30830-4575, USA.

British Library Cataloguing in Publication Data
A catalogue record for this book is available from the
British Library

1-86024-527-7

Cover design by David Lund
Print Management by Adare Carwin
Printed by Haynes, Sparkford, Yeovil, Somerset, UK

Contents

Acknowledgements

This book would never have happened if it weren't for the good people out there who were so enthusiastic about my first book and inspired me to write a follow-up. This new book still needed to be written, though, so I'd like to thank my wife, Monica, for her great patience with me. Of course, without the love, support and understanding from her and the boys it would have been a lot harder.

Thanks to Simon for being the first to read the manuscript (I'll read yours one of these days), to Jony for dreaming up the title and to Derek, Kevin, Fred and Julia for your positive contributions. Special thanks to Malcolm Down and Authentic for supporting me so well on my first book and for Howard Conder and Chris Hill for the great publicity you gave it.

Not being an accredited historian or theologian, I could never have written this book without the inspiration and mysterious workings of the Holy Spirit, the true author, who put the words into my heart and brain and, through my two typing fingers, into my computer. This book is dedicated to you.

Preface

I used to have a dream where I enter a drab, airy room filled with nervous people sitting in a circle on wooden chairs. All eyes turn to me as I creep to the front, then I turn to face them and make my admission, a brave confession after years of denial. *'My name is Steve and I'm a . . . Jew.'*

Why the dream? Well, the fact is that there was some truth in it, brought on by vestiges of shame from deep within my psyche. You see, I was not always upfront about my racial origins, even when confronted by direct questioning. *'But you do look Jewish.'* *'No, not me, mate, you're mistaken.'* I was never sure where this shame came from. Perhaps it was the desire not to be different; perhaps it was a need not to be stereotyped. Or, most likely, perhaps there was fear of rejection, the least serious of the whole gamut of emotions and reactions provoked by making the statement, *'My name is Steve and I'm a . . . Jew.'* Because, let's face it, earlier generations have faced a lot worse than mere rejection.

As far as I could remember, the only thing Jewish about my family was when we gorged ourselves with food at Uncle Syd's at Passover time. We even had a Christmas tree at my Nana's house every year, though I don't recollect us actually going as far as singing carols. In fact, I was the only religious person in my family, as far as I could see. For as long as I could remember, up to my 13th birthday, I was blessed (or cursed?) with the weekly visit of Rabbi Jacobs. He was the one who taught me to be a Jew. I became the world authority on Deuteronomy 12. I could read it forwards and backwards, sing it, even yodel it. My whole reason for being, in a Jewish sense, was to learn that passage until it permeated every pore of my body. And the whole reason behind that was that, on some fateful day in some far-off time, I would be able to stand up in confidence at the front of a synagogue congregation at the time of my bar mitzvah and sing that passage with the unwavering voice of a pre-pubescent Cantor. And the whole reason behind that was that my dad, a few rows ahead of me, and my mum, hidden among the hats in the gallery, could get that warm glow of satisfaction that comes only from the knowledge that you've brought up your son in a proper Jewish manner. That's what being Jewish was to me. I could say that with confidence because, the day after my bar mitzvah, there was no Rabbi Jacobs, no Hebrew lessons, no Deuteronomy 12. At last I didn't have to be Jewish any more; I could be like everyone else!

Deprived of Jewish friends from childhood, having had a private Hebrew tutor, I drifted more towards Gentiles. If it had been up to me I would have hidden my Jewishness under a bush at the school entrance. As things were, my religion was down on the register. I was excused RE and worship in the chapel and given far more interesting things to do, such as learning Braille and corresponding with blind kids. We occasionally had to sit through the odd RE lesson, although, curiously, I can't remember anything about religion being taught. I was friendly with only two of the Jewish boys in my class, one a committed Zionist, no doubt by now a respected settler in Israel, and the other a rabid atheist. The others were more typically Jewish, and at least two of them grew up to become very high achievers. One is now a highly acclaimed QC and the other a nationally known journalist.

At 18 I left for university. Real freedom at last, and this time I did not so much leave my Jewish identity behind as bury it twelve feet underground! It wasn't without a great deal of shame and, later, regret, that I went through my three years at college as a WASP (White Anglo-Saxon Protestant, or, in my case, Weak Anti-Social Person). This was fine until the last month of my last term of my last year, just after Finals, when I inexplicably fell for a Christian girl and was introduced to Jesus, and my life was never to be the same again. But that's another book!

Why should I be ashamed of my heritage? I wasn't alone; I knew of many family friends who had changed their surnames after the Second World War, to distance themselves from the shame of the Holocaust and the realities of post-war anti-Semitism. Would they have done the same if they had been born Greek, or Swedish, or Icelandic? I very much doubt it. Being Jewish has always been a provocation to others around you, whoever they are, whatever period of history you are living in. Don't you find that strange?

It *is* strange, and it really needs to be examined.

Steve Maltz
London, 2004

Introduction

We Jews are a strange people. Buffeted and battered by the forces of history, we survive with our senses intact. Our story is perhaps the saddest of all, yet we have helped to give humour to the world. A race that was being systematically slaughtered by Nazi brutes in Europe was, at the same time, entertaining America on stage and screen. A people who have, on the world stage, produced the highest number of Nobel Prize winners in proportion to their numbers have been persecuted and reviled and forced into ghettoes. A folk who provided Gentiles, in Jesus of Nazareth, with a Saviour and inspiration are tortured and killed in the name of the same man.

Why can't they all just leave us alone – to create, invent, compose and entertain – and find another people to torment? What's it all about? So, the Jews are meant to be different, the 'chosen people'. As Tevye said in *Fiddler on the Roof*, '*Maybe we've had enough of being chosen, Lord; can't you go and choose someone else – if only for one day?'* Do we feel the same way? Does our chosenness mean anything to us now, in the twenty-first century? Sure, it's a source of great pride when we look at the achievements of our people, often against great odds. But we don't like reading and hearing about the other side, the Holocaust and the pogroms. Yet they both work together, they are both part of the same package, like strawberries and cream (or perhaps I should say like smoked salmon and beigels).

Jewish achievements in the world at large are nothing short of astounding. There are just over 13 million Jews worldwide (2000 figures[1]), out of a world population of 6,100 million. This means that about 0.21 per cent of the world is Jewish: about one person out of every 470. So one would naturally expect that about 0.21 per cent of the world's scientists, musicians, entertainers, writers etc. would be Jewish. Well, it hasn't worked out like that; something has gone wrong in our calculations, our decimal point has gone haywire. Just looking at the period since the mid-nineteenth century we find that about 25 per cent of the world's scientists have been Jews. That's over one hundred times too many! It has also been estimated that in 1978, over half the Nobel Prize winners were Jewish.[2] Over 50 per cent of the main contributors to human progress that year came from 0.21 per cent of the population! But has mankind been grateful for this contribution? What do people think of the Jews?

This book has been written to look at how the world has reacted to the Jewish people over the centuries, from the time of Abraham to the modern day. We will be doing this by looking at the names given to them by their enemies, their friends and God himself, and we will be pondering the significance of the Jewish story for the times in which we now live.

'Sticks and stones may break my bones, but names can never harm me.' How wrong can this be if you happen to be Jewish! Names can be harmful indeed, especially when they are also accompanied by sticks, stones and whatever else can be thrown at you.

Jews certainly have been known by a whole library of names, mostly derogatory. Even God Himself wasn't always complimentary, calling them stiff-necked. But He also called them the apple of His eye, and this is significant. What is also significant is that despite all this name-calling, the Jews, by the very fact of surviving for so long, have managed to confound all models of history. The historian Arnold Toynbee, who couldn't fit them into any of the usual moulds, just dismissed them as fossils of history. Oh yes? How many fossils do you know that account for 25 per cent of the world's scientists since the mid-nineteenth century? The Jews are certainly an interesting people.

We will begin by considering the question, who exactly is a Jew? At a time of unprecedented mixing between the races we find ourselves in a society inhabited by folk of all hues and mixtures of traditions. My own children have the culturally confused heritage of English secular Judaism mixed with Polish Catholicism. My wife comes from a German/Polish background; her German mother is an atheist and her Polish father was a Catholic. What does that make our children? According to one definition they are not Jewish by birth, but another tradition would make them as Jewish as they wish to be and yet another tradition, the Nazi one, albeit for the wrong purposes, would make them Jewish on account of their grand-parents' background and nothing else. If you go to Israel and expect to see a nation of olive skin and brown eyes you'll be surprised at the blond hair and blue eyes you'll see, even in that bastion of national identity, the Israeli Army. These days, contrary to the belief of some, you can't measure your Jewishness by the size of your nose. Mind you, I am reminded of the true story of a friend, a Gentile, who discovered only when he was in his twenties that his father was Jewish. His first words at this discovery were, *'Ah, so that explains the nose!'* This story aside, we need a better way of defining Jewishness and we do this in our first chapter, when we look at the question of origins.

But what of today? What do modern Jews think of their identity? There is a certain degree of pride. After all, Jewish people have impacted the world in so many different spheres and have influenced the thinking of the world so dramatically that we need to look deeper at this situation. The three men who have arguably most influenced the twentieth century, Albert Einstein, Sigmund Freud and Karl Marx, were all Jewish, as were the founders of two of the main world religions, Judaism and Christianity. Even Muhammad, the founder of Islam, drew greatly from Jewish sources. I'm sure someday someone will discover that the Buddha was a victim of the first Diaspora who got lost and ended up in India!

Like it or not, we Jews are pretty religious too. There is a joke told in various forms by Jews the world over. It goes something like this, in a heavy Yiddish accent:

Sadie Cohen, an elderly Jewish lady from New York, goes to her travel agent.

'I vont to go to India.'

'Mrs Cohen, India! It's filthy, it's too hot, and it's full of brown people!'

'I vont to go to India.'

'But it's a long journey. And what will you eat? The food's too hot and spicy. You can't drink the water; you can't eat fresh fruit or vegetables. You'll get ill. Plague, cholera, typhoid. God only knows. Can you imagine? And no Jewish doctors. Why torture yourself?'

'I vont to go to India.'

So arrangements are made and off she goes. She gets there and despite the noise, the smells, the crowds, she gets to the ashram, a holy place. There she joins the long queue waiting to see the guru, the holy man. She's told she'll have to queue for three days. Out comes her knitting. Eventually she's at the head of the queue. She's told firmly that she's allowed only three words with the guru.

'Dat's OK.'

She's ushered into the inner sanctum where the guru is seated, ready to bestow blessings on eager disciples. Again she's reminded by an aide that she's only got three words. Unlike every other visitor, she doesn't prostrate herself at his feet. She stands right in front of him, her arms crossed, staring at him fixedly, and says,

'Marvin, come home.'

You may laugh, but Jews form a large proportion of both leaders and followers of many spiritual movements, some of them decidedly dodgy. You'll see them in yoga and meditation classes, New Age cults, Hindu and Buddhist groups. One guru had so many Jewish disciples that he called them 'Hinjews'. Jews are not always as materially minded as people think; many seem to spend their lives searching to fill a spiritual 'hole in their heart'.

So, what is special about this folk? And where does it say that these people are special, chosen for some purpose? Where does it say *'all peoples on earth will be blessed through you'*? The Bible, of course. How could the writers of the Bible have known about Einstein, Freud and Marx (though it's hard to discern what sort of blessing we received here, considering the fruits of their endeavours – the atom bomb, overpaid psychiatrists and communism), to say nothing of the scores of other major influences? How could they know about this 'one solitary life', the Jew Jesus, written about in a famous essay?

'Here is a man who was born in an obscure village, the child of a peasant woman. He grew up in another village. He worked in a carpenter shop until he was thirty, and then for three years he was an itinerant preacher. He never owned a home. He never wrote a book. He never held an office. He never had a family. He never went to college. He never put his foot inside a big city. He never travelled more

than two hundred miles from the place where he was born. He never did one of the things that usually accompany greatness. He had no credentials but himself . . . I am far within the mark when I say that all the armies that ever marched, all the navies that ever were built; all the parliaments that ever sat and all the kings that ever reigned, put together, have not affected the life of man upon this earth as powerfully as has that one solitary life.'[3]

Like it or not, the above is true, though the effects felt by the Jewish nation as a result of this particular 'solitary life' have been one of the tragedies of history, a subject that we will explore in later chapters.

NOTES

1 Source: Jewish Virtual Library http://www.jewishvirtuallibrary. org/jsource/History/worldpop.html for Jewish statistics, US Census Bureau http://www.census.gov/ipc/www/worldpop. html for world statistics.
2 More information about Jewish Nobel Prize winners can be found at SimpleToRemember.com, http://www.simpleto remember.com/vitals/JewishNobelPrizeWinners.html
3 This essay was adapted from a sermon by Dr James Allan Francis in *The Real Jesus and Other Sermons* © 1926 The Judson Press of Philadelphia (pp 123–4, entitled 'Arise Sir Knight!').

Prologue

It was an amazing deal, the likes of which had never been offered to a group of people before and would never be offered again. These people had already been through a lot, both good and bad. They had spent their whole lives wandering and wondering. It had been far worse for their parents. They had grown up as slaves and had died in sadness, their potential unrealised, in the unforgiving desert. That whole generation, bar two, had now perished and here we find their children standing on the threshold of a new chapter in their lives.

They had trudged around the desert for up to forty years, yet things could have been far worse. They had a ready supply of food and water, their clothes had not worn out and not one of them had suffered so much as a blister on their feet. And they were bolstered by tales of great miracles, involving the parting of mighty waters, remarkable deliverances from their enemies, and everyday provisions. And they didn't travel alone; their God travelled with them. The God who had created them and the world in which they lived had chosen to lead them personally, through a vanguard of cloud and fire. And this same God now offered them a new deal.

It was to be an end of their fruitless wanderings. A land was being offered to them. A land where they could settle, their lifelong travels finally at an end. A land with streams and refreshing valley springs. A land with wheat and barley, vines and fig trees, pomegranates, olive oil and honey. A rich land, where copper and iron were easily mined. A land where they would lack nothing. And best of all, it would be handed to them on a plate. Vineyards and olive groves would already be established, wells already dug, and large flourishing cities would be theirs, as vacant possession.

Their leader, 120 years old, surveyed this Promised Land from a high place with sadness in his heart. He knew that his days were numbered, that he was on the threshold of death, never to lead his people into this land of milk and honey. But his sadness was not for himself, but rather for the people he had led for forty years. He knew something they didn't. He knew that these blessings would never be fully realised by his people and he knew why.

You see, there were conditions attached, simple conditions. God had offered them a choice between life and prosperity on the one hand, and death and destruction on the other. To claim the former all they had to do was to love him, walk in his ways and keep his laws. This should not have been difficult, partly because these laws were there for their protection, safety and well-being. They were to deserve the latter if they ignored these instructions, followed their own ways and turned towards the gods of the people already in the land.

They were offered life or death, blessings or curses. Choose life, pleaded the God who wanted to give them the world, but they didn't listen. True, they entered the Promised Land and began to conquer it and to enjoy the blessings offered. But they chose the dark side, seduced by the gods and customs of the native people. As a consequence, they took around a thousand years to fully conquer the land, then proceeded to lose the lot before being exiled from the land itself, condemned to wander the world right up to the modern era.

Such has been the lot of the Jews. Offered so much, but still going their own way. No wonder they were called a stiff-necked people. The story of Moses and the children of Israel is not just a cautionary tale, a fable conjured up by the human imagination. The story is from the pages of the world's best-selling book, the Bible. It is from the fifth section, originally titled 'Words', but saddled with the title 'Deuteronomy', a name taken from an alien culture hundreds of years after the events took place.

This is the point where we take a deep breath and discuss our frames of reference before we go any further. The Bible – that's my frame of reference. But I can't just leave it at that, as many have looked into that particular book and seen different things. So what do I see there? I see a book that speaks from God's mind to our mind and God's heart to our heart. Whether or not you believe in God is not the issue here; that's between you and Him. Whatever your background, all I ask you to do is consider the possibility that there is a God, who chooses to communicate to us through the Bible.

If you're one of those who view the Bible as a relic from history, with no more credibility in the real world than *The Hobbit*, I may be asking you to take a step in faith. But the fact remains that this is the best place to start to examine early Jewish history. Even if you consider it more fiction than fact, it is the Bible, usually in the hands of other people, that has done more to shape Jewish history than anything else.

In the view of many, the Bible's explanation is the only one that makes sense of the history of the Jewish people to the present day. Political, historical and sociological analysis gets us nowhere on this issue. Jews are an anomaly – mere fossils according to the historian Toynbee, as mentioned earlier. Most would say that it was the Bible that got them in the mess in the first place, but what the Bible also does is offer hope that everything that has happened to them has been for a purpose, and that there is a very real possibility of a happy ending.

So, let's begin at the beginning . . .

Chapter 1

The Children of the Promise

The story is really quite straightforward. God wanted to give humanity a chance after they'd blown it when Adam and Eve ate from the forbidden tree. He had a plan and, to carry out this plan, He needed one people out of all the nations who would be *His* people. But where would He find this people? He had to start somewhere so He chose one man, Abraham. Perhaps he was the latest of a long list, the others having failed in the selection process. We don't know, and the Bible doesn't tell us, but it does tell us how Abraham found himself in that privileged position.

Abraham (then called Abram) was chosen by God while he was living in Ur of the Chaldees, his homeland, around 4,000 years ago. A Jewish legend[1] speaks of his father, Terah, as an idol-maker and says that even when he was still young, Abram realised that idol worship was nothing but foolishness. To make his point, one day, when Abram was asked to mind the shop, he took a hammer and smashed all the idols – except for the largest. His father came home aghast. *'What happened?'* he shouted. *'It was amazing, Dad,'* replied Abram. *'The idols all got into a fight and the biggest idol won!'* This must surely have been pleasing to God, who later spoke to him when he was living in Haran.

> 'The LORD had said to Abram, "Leave your country, your people and your father's household and go to the land I will show you. I will make you into a great nation and I will bless you; I will make your name great, and you will be a blessing. I will bless those who bless you, and whoever curses you I will curse; and all peoples on earth will be blessed through you"' (Gen. 12:1–3).

The fact that Abram did what he was asked and moved to the area of Canaan, modern-day Israel, marked him down as a man willing to listen to the voice of God. He exercised the same faith as his ancestor Noah, who, ten generations earlier, had built a large boat at God's command, even though he was miles from the sea and despite the ridicule of those around him. It takes great faith indeed to follow God's commands when it seems to go against all natural logic and takes you far away from the comfort zone of your everyday life. Abram's faith muscles were stirred into life, but they were going to have to be flexed to breaking point soon.

'Abram, your offspring will be like the dust of the earth . . .'

'How so? I am childless.'

'A son from your own body will be your heir . . .'

Look at this through Abram's eyes. He was getting on a bit, perhaps in his eighties already. His wife, Sarai, had never borne children, so it was unlikely that she was going to start now. But Genesis 15:6 gives Abram's response to God's promise:

'Abram believed the LORD . . .'

That was good enough for God, very pleasing in fact. His reaction was this:

'. . . and he credited it to him as righteousness.'

Abram's reaction put him into credit with God. He had done the right thing.

But before we put Abram on too high a pedestal, we realise that even he had his flaws. Perhaps quite a few years had passed since this great act of faith and the old bones were creaking a bit. After all, he was around 86 years old now, when Sarai said to him, 'It's not happening, is it, dear?' No child had yet burst forth from her loins.

> 'Now Sarai, Abram's wife, had borne him no children. But she had an Egyptian maidservant named Hagar; so she said to Abram, "The LORD has kept me from having children. Go, sleep with my maidservant; perhaps I can build a family through her." Abram agreed to what Sarai said' (Gen. 16:1–2).

So he slept with Hagar, produced a child, Ishmael, and through this act of impatience laid the foundations for the current Middle Eastern conflict, over 4,000 years later! More of that later.

But God wasn't going to give up on him, and thirteen years later He confirmed Abram's status in two very visible ways. Firstly, He changed his name to *Abraham*, meaning 'father of many', as a further reminder of His earlier promise that his offspring would be like the dust of the earth. Secondly, He instituted the rite of circumcision. Much squealing must have been heard in camp on the day Abraham and his son were circumcised. He didn't have the benefit of anaesthetic or the trusting nature of an 8-day-old baby! Abraham was 99 years old when he was snipped. And no men in his household escaped this ordeal, not even foreign servants. They were all put to the blade. It was to be a visible reminder from that day onwards that Abraham and his descendants belonged to God in a special way.

Sarai, too, was blessed by a name change, though with it was a reminder that perhaps sleeping with Hagar wasn't going to be the way that God had in mind when

He spoke of Abraham's offspring. Her name was changed to *Sarah*, with these words: '*I will bless her and will surely give you a son by her. I will bless her so that she will be the mother of nations; kings of peoples will come from her*' (Gen. 17:16).

That made Abraham laugh so much, he fell over. A child at the age of 100? And Sarah's 90 years old! He was troubled about Ishmael, now 13. What was to happen with him? It was then that God made very clear His intentions.

Abraham was going to be the father of two distinct peoples. The first would be descended from Ishmael. He would found a dynasty of twelve rulers and be made into a great nation. But it would be with the second people that God would establish his covenant: '. . . *your wife Sarah will bear you a son, and you will call him Isaac. I will establish my covenant with him as an everlasting covenant for his descendants after him*' (Gen. 17:19).

The next year Sarah gave birth to Isaac and we hear nothing of the boy until, a number of years later, God speaks again to Abraham: '*Then God said, "Take your son, your only son, Isaac, whom you love, and go to the region of Moriah. Sacrifice him there as a burnt offering on one of the mountains I will tell you about"*' (Gen. 22:2).

It was to be a test. It was a test of Abraham's faith. Would God really destroy the very son to whom He had earlier promised an everlasting covenant for his descendants after him? Abraham passed this test with flying colours; he even had the knife poised in his hand, ready to deal the fatal blow to his beloved son. God stopped him at the eleventh hour and again carved a notch on the faith-pole. Abraham showed the most amazing faith in God here, outweighing any lapses he may have had earlier in his eventful life. He was so sure of God's promises that he actually believed God would raise Isaac from the dead, even though he had never witnessed such a deed.

This is true faith, and it is no wonder that Abraham became the father of a great dynasty.

'I will make you into a great nation and I will bless you; I will make your name great, and you will be a blessing. I will bless those who bless you, and whoever curses you I will curse; and all peoples on earth will be blessed through you' (Gen. 12:2–3).

Isaac grew up and married the beautiful Rebekah, a distant relative. We read little about him, but we are told much about the life and times of his son, Jacob.

Jacob and Esau were twins but were hardly bosom buddies. They even fought in the womb. God offered an explanation for this, describing how their futures and the futures of their descendants were going to be very different.

'Two nations are in your womb, and two peoples from within you will be separated; one people will be stronger than the other, and the older will serve the younger' (Gen. 25:23).

Esau became the manly one, the older and the stronger, a hunter by profession. Jacob, the younger by a few minutes, was the clever, craftier one. He was quiet and preferred to hang around at home with mother. But he was a good cook and, interestingly, it was through his excellent red stew that the above prophecy would start to come to pass. A starving Esau, after a hard day's hunting, sold his precious birthright to Jacob for a bowl of this stew, followed by some bread, then another stew of lentils. It obviously meant little to him, but it meant more to Jacob, who took this to the next stage when Isaac, their father, was coming to the end of his life.

Urged on by his scheming mother, Jacob tricked Isaac into giving him the blessing due to Esau as the first-born.

You'll have to read the account yourself in Genesis 27 to find out what happened but, needless to say, food was involved, as before. This is a curious episode, as Esau had already forfeited his right to this blessing in the earlier incident, so all Jacob was doing was claiming what was rightfully his, even if it was bought for the price of a bowl of stew!

This was the blessing that Isaac gave to Jacob:

'May nations serve you and peoples bow down to you. Be lord over your brothers, and may the sons of your mother bow down to you. May those who curse you be cursed and those who bless you be blessed' (Gen. 27:29).

And so the prophecy over the womb was fulfilled. We shall see a little later how this all panned out, historically speaking.

Jacob then ran away from home, fearful at what Esau might do to him for stealing the blessing. He escaped to his uncle Laban, but on the way had an encounter with God, at a place called Bethel. There he dreamt of the stairway to heaven and God spoke to him, repeating all the promises made to his grandfather Abraham and father Isaac. It was a clear sign that the Lord God was blessing him and was with him, even though he was now in exile from the land of his fathers.

He was, however, a flawed character and decided to set his own conditions on his relationship with God, even though God's promises to him were entirely uncondi-tional. The gist of it was this: OK, God, if you stay with me and if you look after me on this journey and if you give me food to eat and if you give me clothes to wear, then . . . you can be my God.

God must have chuckled at the cheek of it, but had the last laugh when Jacob subsequently managed to dig himself into a hole and stayed there for fourteen years. First he was betrothed to Laban's beautiful daughter Rachel, in return for seven years' work as a shepherd. On the wedding night he was tricked into marrying Leah, the less physically alluring daughter, and only found out in the morning, either because he was too drunk the night before to notice or, perhaps, because she was veiled and it was dark! The only way he could also marry the beautiful Rachel was to work there for another seven years. During that time his love life was interesting, to say the least, as he had relations not only with Leah and Rachel, but also with their respective servants. There was even a comical episode when Rachel hired him out to Leah for a night of passion in return for exotic fruit.

The result of these liaisons was twelve sons and a daughter, Dinah. Six of the sons – Reuben, Simeon, Levi, Judah, Issachar and Zebulun – were from Leah, and two – Joseph and Benjamin – were from Rachel. The other four – Dan, Naphtali, Gad and Asher – were from the maidservants.

Eventually Jacob fell out with Laban over some sheep and decided to leave him. God spoke to him and told him that it was now time to return to the land of his fathers, Canaan. But first he needed to make his peace with his estranged brother, Esau. This filled him with fear and trepidation, so he needed to know that there would be a measure of divine help in this enterprise.

'Then Jacob prayed, "O God of my father Abraham, God of my father Isaac, O LORD, who said to me, 'Go back to your country and your relatives, and I will make you prosper,' I am unworthy of all the kindness and faithfulness you have shown your servant. I had only my staff when I crossed this Jordan, but now I have become two groups. Save me, I pray, from the hand of my brother Esau, for I am afraid he will come and attack me, and also the mothers with their children. But you have said, 'I will

surely make you prosper and will make your descendants like the
sand of the sea, which cannot be counted'" ' (Gen. 32:9–12).

God's response was swift and unexpected. He took Jacob on in an all-night wrestling bout. It appears that the only way Jacob could be overpowered was by having his hip dislocated. Even then Jacob refused to let go unless he was blessed.

'Your name will no longer be Jacob, but Israel, because you
have struggled with God and with men and have overcome'
(Gen. 32:28).

Israel, meaning 'he struggles with God', was his new name, and a new chapter in the history of humanity's relationship with God now began. *Israel*. It's a strange name really, if you think about it. Here was a favoured dynasty, formed from the twelve sons of Jacob, who would become a nation. Yet they were given a name not to indicate any special favour in a positive sense, but one that highlights their one consistent character trait, as the story unfolds through the Bible. Israel – *struggles with God*. For a chosen, privileged people you would have expected a gentler name, such as *listens to God*, or *follows God*. But *struggles with God*? What's this all about? What it tells us, and told them too, was that it wasn't going to be a bed of roses. God didn't choose a compliant, holier-than-holy people who would be His lap dogs and willing servants in days to come. Instead He chose a real, flawed people representative of all humanity. A people named after Jacob for good reason. He wasn't perfect, he wasn't always a man of faith and he forced God to bless him on more than one occasion. In many ways he was like you and me.

Let's look back now and summarise where we have got to in our story.

Abraham was the one who found favour with God. He showed great faith, first by obeying the call and moving to an unknown land, then by accepting that he was to become a father despite his advancing years, and finally by being willing to sacrifice his son in the sure hope that he would be brought back to life in order to fulfil God's promises of descendants like 'the dust of the earth', 'becoming a great nation'.

He had two sons, Ishmael and Isaac, but it was the younger who would inherit these promises, just as it would be with his grandchildren, when Jacob, the younger twin, would go on to gain the blessings and provide descendants *'like the sand of the sea, which cannot be counted'*.

And what of the older brothers? Well, true to the prophecy, Ishmael had twelve sons, who became twelve tribal rulers. It is said that they lived in hostility towards all their brothers, a situation that sadly seems to have continued right up to the present day, with Muslim Arabs in their current conflict with Israeli Jews. Esau, also called Edom, supposedly after the red stew that led to his downfall, became the father of the Edomites in the hill country. These people were to become a thorn in the side of the descendants of Jacob, particularly through the descendants of Amalek, whom God later urged His people to blot out.

So God's chosen family line was Abraham, Isaac and Jacob. We see God identifying Himself over thirty times in the Bible as the God of Abraham, Isaac and Jacob. He was making a point. It wasn't Abraham, Ishmael and Nebaioth, or Abraham, Isaac and Esau. Interestingly, this blessed line consisted of second sons, not first-borns. Neither Isaac nor Jacob was the first-fruits of his father's loins. Just being the first-born guarantees you nothing in God's eyes, and an interesting verse in Malachi illustrates this graphically:

'"*Was not Esau Jacob's brother?*" the LORD says. "*Yet I have loved Jacob, but Esau I have hated . . .*"' (Mal. 1:2–3).

This is a bit extreme, isn't it? It's just unfamiliar use of language, showing the gap between the ancient Jewish culture and ours. What is meant here is to emphasise God's love of Jacob, by lessening His regard for Esau. In our terms we would say that He 'loved Esau less'.

The blessed line follows through to the next generation, to the sons of Jacob, or, as they are more commonly known, the children of Israel. Again we are surprised in that God doesn't choose the first-born son to continue the line. Neither does He choose the second-born, nor the third-born. It's the fourth-born, Judah, who carries the blessings to the next generation. Reuben, the eldest, forfeited his blessing by sleeping with his stepmother. The other two, Simeon and Levi, had too violent a nature (they slaughtered all the men in a city in revenge for the rape of their sister) to be trusted with a divine mandate. But Judah received the following blessing:

'The sceptre will not depart from Judah, nor the ruler's staff from between his feet, until he comes to whom it belongs and the obedience of the nations is his' (Gen. 49:10).

It is interesting to observe that up to this point God meanders through the family line. He chose Isaac, but not Ishmael. He chose Jacob, but not Esau. The discards go off and found other nations who from then on are outside the purposes of God. But then we arrive at the twelve sons of Jacob, the children of Israel, and we see a nation being founded. All twelve sons produce family lines, but all stay within God's chosen nation. In fact they grow together and cement themselves as a distinct people, the Hebrews, in the nation of Egypt, arriving as honoured guests of the Pharaoh thanks to their rejected brother Joseph, but living most of their lives there as slaves to subsequent Egyptian rulers.

We read that around seventy of the children of Israel made this journey into Egypt. They entered as an extended family, but left, 430 years later, as the Hebrew nation of around 2.5 million. The name *Hebrew* possibly derives from Eber, an early ancestor of Abraham, though it's unclear why. A more natural name for these people would be Abrahamites, or Abites, but who are we to question the vagaries of history? Another name for them was *Israelites*, which made a bit more sense.

This was the Exodus, the most momentous event in Jewish history, commemorated yearly at the Passover festival. It was here that God made His first great entrance in corporate human history, through the provision of a whole symphony of miracles and mighty deeds. He also introduced Himself to Moses through the burning bush. The God of Abraham, Isaac and Jacob revealed His personal name, the name passed down to us as *Yahveh* or *Jehovah* and translated as 'I am who I am'.

Moses led the children of Israel to Mount Sinai and it was there that they were consecrated for service, as we read:

> 'Then Moses went up to God, and the LORD called to him from the mountain and said, "This is what you are to say to the house of Jacob and what you are to tell the people of Israel: 'You yourselves have seen what I did to Egypt, and how I carried you on eagles' wings and brought you to myself. Now if you obey me fully and keep my covenant, then out of all nations you will be my treasured possession. Although the whole earth is mine, you will be for me a kingdom of priests and a holy nation.' These are the words you are to speak to the Israelites' (Ex. 19:3–6).

The decision was theirs. They could have turned down the offer. But they accepted their role and cemented a special relationship with God that has lasted to the present day.

> *'The people all responded together, "We will do everything the* LORD *has said"'* (Ex. 19:8).

The relationship may have been made in heaven, but it was always going to be a bumpy ride.

We have learnt that . . .
The Jews were still called Hebrews or the children of Israel at this time. They had been freed by God, through Moses, from captivity in Egypt and we see them for the first time as a new nation, just about to discover its destiny.

NOTES

1 From *Midrash Rabbah* 38:13.

Chapter 2

The Kingdom of Priests

'The people all responded together, "We will do everything the
LORD has said"' (Ex.19:8).

They may have meant what they said at the time, or
perhaps they just said what Moses wanted to hear.
Nevertheless, they were accepting their God-given role as
the *kingdom of priests* and a *holy nation*. But what, exactly,
were they letting themselves in for?

It's awesome if you think about it. A priest is someone
who interacts with God on behalf of his people. It is his job
to make sure that all is right between them and God. They
had taken on a role of breathtaking importance, God's
people on earth. If they had known in advance the places
this relationship would take them in later years, they
would have made a beeline back to Egyptian slavery,
there and then.

They were to become humanity's representatives to
God almighty. Of the scores of peoples and nations
scattered through the earth at that time, from the Chinese
in the far east to the Egyptians in the west, it was this
bedraggled band of ex-slaves who had been chosen as a

channel for God's dealings with humanity. He chose them not because they were the largest nation, or the nicest people, or the cleverest folk, or the most moral of human beings. He chose them because He is God and He chooses whom He chooses. He chose them for a role that promised both blessings and curses, depending on decisions that they would make. He gave them a burden that, frankly, was going to be a millstone round their necks, and other nations should feel eternally grateful that it was the Jewish people that were chosen and not any other. He chose them, knowing full well that they were initially going to fail:

> *'And the* LORD *said to Moses: "You are going to rest with your fathers, and these people will soon prostitute themselves to the foreign gods of the land they are entering. They will forsake me and break the covenant I made with them. On that day I will become angry with them and forsake them; I will hide my face from them, and they will be destroyed. Many disasters and difficulties will come upon them, and on that day they will ask, 'Have not these disasters come upon us because our God is not with us?' And I will certainly hide my face on that day because of all their wickedness in turning to other gods"' (Deut. 31:16–18).*

He knew they were going to fail, not because they were the most insignificant nation, or the nastiest people, or a bunch of idiots, or the most immoral of folk. He knew they were going to fail because they were human beings: in terms of what warms the heart of God we are all doomed to failure. The Jewish people were no different in that respect from what the Egyptians or Chinese or Hittites would have been. It's no use condemning them for their failure, just as it is no use castigating them for their rejection of Jesus; they were just doing exactly what you and I would have done.

God may have known in advance that His kingdom of priests would fail, but He did all He could to help them succeed. This is why He made them a holy nation. The original meaning of the word *holy* can be a surprise to some. It implies being *apart from others*. If someone is *holy*, it doesn't mean they are morally, spiritually or ethically pure; what it really means is that he or she tries to live a life separated from the uncleanliness of the rest of us. This is a person apart. The Jewish people were a people apart, kept apart by the laws and customs imposed on them by God for a purpose.

These people were together, separated from the rest of humanity, for forty years in the wilderness. It was meant to be a brief trip in the sun, but turned into an extended nightmare because of their impatience and faithlessness. Early on they were at Kadesh, surveying the land promised to them by God, the 'land of milk and honey'. They sent spies to check things out, but then chose to believe wildly exaggerated reports of giants and powerful cities rather than the measured report of Joshua and Caleb. Although these two didn't deny the hardships that might be ahead of them, they stated that if God were truly with them, they would surely take the land, end of story. For this declaration of faith the people even considered stoning them! No wonder God was angered; He struck down the whingeing spies with a plague and condemned the whole assembly to a forty-year marathon in the desert, never to know rest.

This experience nevertheless had the effect of forging these people together as a nation. God shepherded them and strengthened them, binding them together through the *Torah*, the instructions for life given to Moses at Sinai. This was a set of 613 rules and regulations designed not just to unite them as a people under God but also to provide them with rules for living and surviving in those times, covering issues of behaviour, diet, relationships and much more. *Torah*, often labelled in a negative sense as 'law', was intended to be viewed in a positive light as teachings or instructions.

The uniqueness of this people is seen when we consider the sequence of events that accompanied the beginning of their conquest of the 'Promised Land'. Firstly, God provided a miracle by parting the River Jordan – no bridges for this army! To emphasise the divine nature of this event, the huge army was to cross the river not by a direct route, but fanned out to the north and south. This was because the centre of the river was taken up by the priests carrying the Ark of the Covenant – God's earthly home – and no one else was allowed to pass within 900 metres of this, on pain of death.

Next, the Jewish men were circumcised with flint knives! Circumcision was the most important sign of who they were. It was an instruction given to Abraham hundreds of years earlier.

> *'You are to undergo circumcision, and it will be the sign of the covenant between me and you. For the generations to come every male among you who is eight days old must be circumcised, including those born in your household or bought with money from a foreigner – those who are not your offspring. Whether born in your household or bought with your money, they must be circumcised. My covenant in your flesh is to be an everlasting covenant. Any uncircumcised male, who has not been circumcised in the flesh, will be cut off from his people; he has broken my covenant' (Gen. 17:11–14).*

What had happened was that during the forty years in the desert (perhaps even earlier), the children of Israel had stopped circumcising their children. Perhaps God was sparing them extra pain, their trudging endlessly through the desert being punishment enough. Perhaps it was simply because, as they were separated from the rest of the world during that time, there was no one around for them to display a sign on their body to. But crunch time had now come; they were about to re-enter the world and meet other nations. They now had to display a sign of their separateness, their holiness. They had to go under the knife; there was no escape.

Then they partook of the Passover meal, a commemoration of that event forty years earlier when their parents (mostly) had taken their first step of nationhood and left behind their lives in Egypt. The Passover commemoration was part of the *Torah* instructions given by God, as described in Numbers 9:2: *'Make the Israelites celebrate the Passover at the appointed time.'*

This was an important Passover meal for them. It was the first they had ever celebrated as free people in a land of their own, and the day after they ate of the produce of this land, the manna that had sustained them for decades in the desert suddenly ceased falling from the sky. A new chapter had started.

Finally, Joshua was to meet an angel on the road to Jericho, who told him how this walled city was to be taken by the Israelites. Priests with trumpets were going to pave the way for this particular siege, and you know the rest of the story. If you don't, then suffice it to say that they marched round the walls of the city and, as an encore, 'brought the house down'.

Yes, this was no ordinary army!

Joshua spent the rest of his life leading his people through battle after battle in this land promised by God, but nevertheless a land already occupied by Canaanites, Amorites, Anakites, Hittites, Perizzites, Hivites and Jebusites. When he was an old man, God informed him that although they had by no means conquered the whole country, it was time to colonise the cities and regions that were in their control. So the twelve tribes of Israel were each allocated a district to call their own and they were given a time to enjoy the peace. Joshua was even older when he gathered together the great and the good from the tribes and made what was, by all accounts, his farewell speech:

> *'You yourselves have seen everything the LORD your God has done to all these nations for your sake; it was the LORD your God who fought for you' (Josh. 23:3).*

He needed to remind them that they weren't by nature great military tacticians. They hadn't graduated from a middle-eastern West Point or Sandhurst. They were basically just upstart slaves who had become desert nomads. Their success was due to the simple fact that they were representatives on earth of the God of the universe and He wasn't going to let them fail to conquer the land He had promised them. And it was important that they shouldn't forget this important fact. Joshua reminded them:

> *'The LORD has driven out before you great and powerful nations; to this day no-one has been able to withstand you. One of you routs a thousand, because the LORD your God fights for you, just as he promised. So be very careful to love the LORD your God' (Josh. 29:9–10).*

Then the crunch. A warning that, sadly, became an epitaph . . .

> *'But if you turn away and ally yourselves with the survivors of these nations that remain among you and if you intermarry with them and associate with them, then you may be sure that the LORD your God will no longer drive out these nations before you.*

Instead, they will become snares and traps for you, whips on your backs and thorns in your eyes, until you perish from this good land, which the LORD your God has given you' (Josh. 23:12–14).

While Joshua and his generation lived, all went well. These were people who had walked in the presence of God, even if it amounted to travelling around in circles in the Sinai desert. These were people who were God-soaked to the core of their being, benefiting from His provisions and guidance, but also witnessing the penalties for misdemeanours – whether through plague, snake-bites or sudden earthquakes. They knew the score and, as crude as it may seem to our 'sophisticated' twenty-first century eyes, they were a people who needed to be moulded from scratch. So, when they left the desert for the Promised Land they looked to God and Him alone for guidance and leadership. He went before them in battle and they had great successes as a result.

But the next generation was indifferent to God and what He had done for them. They went over to the 'dark side' and started to pay an unhealthy attention to the nations that coexisted with them in the Promised Land. Exotic women, foreign ways and alien gods were their downfall and God was not pleased. As a result, they began to realise that they weren't so good at fighting after all, and every time they went into battle they lost and suffered the consequences.

'Whenever Israel went out to fight, the hand of the LORD was against them to defeat them, just as he had sworn to them. They were in great distress' (Judg. 2:15).

What short memories these people had. It was just as well that God didn't give up on them. He had simply invested too much time in them, developing them as a holy nation, a nation apart. He used these other nations to test them, and although by and large they failed miserably, God was always on hand to offer them new ways to redeem themselves. He raised up a fine line of Judges, from Deborah to Samson. These great men and women of God led them back to the straight and narrow and reminded them of their destiny by leading them into great victories against their enemies. And to remind them all of the supernatural nature of these victories, He made it impossible, in some cases, for them to believe otherwise. In the case of Gideon, the army that was sent out to face the Midianites in battle was led by the most insignificant chap in camp (Gideon himself). Moreover, he whittled it down in numbers – by filtering out the cowards and those who didn't drink their water like dogs – so that no one could have any doubt that this army would have problems routing a tea party, let alone an enemy numbering in their tens of thousands.

The decline was seemingly unstoppable. Prompted by the basic human instincts of pride and independence and influenced by the dodgy lifestyles of the nations that surrounded them, the people of God kept forgetting about the One who had rescued them from Egyptian slavery, fed and sustained them in the desert and given them victory after victory against their enemies. There was the odd acknowledgement. In the story of Ruth we read of God providing food for His people, indicating that at least there were some in leadership in that day who remembered Him and asked for help. This was the tragedy of it all. God was always there, very willing and very, very able to help His kingdom of priests in all circumstances. All they had to do was ask. After all, as we are reminded, it was life He was offering. *Choose life*, He had told them, so that you and your children may live. Incredibly, for the most part they chose death and a life of independence and idolatry. To illustrate the point, let's see what happened to them when they came against the Philistines, their most persistent foes in those days.

'The Philistines deployed their forces to meet Israel, and as the battle spread, Israel was defeated by the Philistines, who killed about four thousand of them on the battlefield' (1 Sam. 4:2).

'How can that be?' cried the elders of Israel. *'Why did the LORD bring defeat upon us?'* This was the right question to ask, as it acknowledged who pulled the strings in matters of war. The right thing to ask next would have been, *'Perhaps we didn't ask Him to help us,'* but they didn't, probably because of the shame they felt for going so far away from their God, the Ruler of the universe. So instead they did what they imagined was the next best thing. They performed an act that illustrated how they had been corrupted by living among foreign people with foreign gods. They provided concrete proof of the need for a 'holy' people to remain separated from corrupting influences and perhaps, also, we can get an inkling of why God repeatedly urged the Israelites to obliterate the corrupt Canaanite tribes in the land. So what did they do, already? Let's read from 1 Samuel 4:3.

'Let us bring the ark of the LORD'S covenant from Shiloh, so that it may go with us and save us from the hand of our enemies.'

Influenced by the pagan beliefs of the Canaanites, they believed that God's power lay in the Ark of the Covenant, rather than in God Himself. They placed their faith in a created object, just as the pagans did, with their Astarte poles and Baal statues. The whole plan backfired and their idolatry, ironically, was their undoing. The news that the Israelites had brought their 'god' to battle inspired the

Philistines to fight even harder. The Israelites lost 30,000 men in battle and the Ark of the Covenant was captured. *'The glory has departed from Israel,'* was the cry. A telling epitaph to this story was what happened to the Philistines as a result of their actions. The Ark became a curse for them. First it caused the physical destruction of their god, Dagon (the idol lost its head and hands), and then the Philistines were overrun with plagues until the Ark was later gladly returned to the Israelites.

A kingdom of priests. We must keep reminding ourselves of this. However badly they behaved and however unpriestlike their actions were, they couldn't escape their destiny. But God knew that, much as He wanted his people to succeed, most wouldn't. Yet his *holy nation* had to endure, in order for His plans to come to pass. Central to His plan was the original promise given to Abraham.

> *'I will make you into a great nation and I will bless you; I will make your name great, and you will be a blessing. I will bless those who bless you, and whoever curses you I will curse; and **all peoples on earth will be blessed through you**' (Gen. 12:2–3 my emphasis).*

For this blessing to be fulfilled, a descendant of Abraham was to come onto the scene at some future date. The patriarch Jacob spoke of him just before his death, when he blessed each of his sons in turn. His special blessing was for his fourth-born son, Judah, from whom we get the name *Jew.*

> *'The sceptre will not depart from Judah, nor the ruler's staff from between his feet, until he comes to whom it belongs and the obedience of the nations is his' (Gen. 49:10).*

The children of Israel were going to be sifted, and God

was going to be ruthless both in preserving the family of
Judah and discarding others who had the misfortune of
being born in the wrong family. It might sound cruel to
our sense of fairness, but it is God's way. It's called the
mystery of election, which is, simply put, the fact that God
chooses whom He chooses for His purposes. He doesn't
choose those who attract His eye or who please Him,
rather He chooses first and it's an added bonus for Him if
they do subsequently manage to please Him. Abraham
certainly pleased Him, though it's hard to see God
receiving much joy from Jacob. But He loved them both on
the basis of His divine choice. The mystery of election
dictated that a future ruler of Israel, who would have *the
obedience of the nations*, would come from the family of
Judah – the *Jew*ish family. So it is no surprise that God's
sifting process should begin as early in the life of the new
nation being forged in the Promised Land as at the time of
the first king, Saul. When he was mustering an army
against the Ammonites, it was reported that the men of
Israel numbered 300,000 and the men of *Judah* numbered
30,000. Already Judah was being set apart from the other
tribes, who were lumped together as *Israel*. Remember,
this was many years before the time of David, Solomon
and the splitting of the country into the Northern and
Southern Kingdoms. But I am getting ahead of myself. . . .

It was the time of Saul, the first king. The people
wanted a king for a very good reason. It's the same reason
why human beings throughout history have tried to do
things their own way and have followed their human
instincts in building their own empires and kingdoms. It's
because we are wilful beings and, when push comes to
shove, quite faithless. We still find it hard to trust God (or
even believe in Him these days) and, rather than waiting
on Him, we go ahead with our own plans, expecting His
blessing when we have spent all our energy and return to

Him with a pleading heart to put things right. So it was with the children of Israel when Saul led them against the Ammonites. They had more faith in a flesh-and-blood, mortal, flawed king than they had in the Lord God, Creator of the universe, who had delivered them from slavery in Egypt, sustained them in the desert and fought on their behalf as they began to conquer the land. The prophet Samuel reminded them exactly *who* was in charge:

> 'But when you saw that Nahash king of the Ammonites was moving against you, you said to me, "No, we want a king to rule over us" – even though the LORD your God was your king. Now here is the king you have chosen, the one you asked for; see, the LORD has set a king over you' (1 Sam. 12:12–13).

And as a further reminder, he called on the Lord to send thunder and rain and declare His majesty. *'And you will realise what an evil thing you did in the eyes of the LORD when you asked for a king,'* he added (verse 17).

It's the old chestnut of faith versus works, putting ourselves and our labours before a complete and sincere trust in God. It is further illustrated by another episode in the life of Saul. All he had to do was assemble his army at Gilgal to face the Philistines, then wait for Samuel to turn up and call on the Lord to be with them. But he didn't wait for Samuel and made the necessary sacrifices himself. He lacked faith and instead decided to act. As a result Samuel, who did eventually turn up, declared:

> 'You acted foolishly ... You have not kept the command the LORD your God gave you; if you had, he would have established your kingdom over Israel for all time. But now your kingdom will not endure; the LORD has sought out a man after his own heart and appointed him leader of his people, because you have not kept the LORD's command' (1 Sam. 13:13–14).

Doh! Saul blew it and prepared the way for his successor, David. His dynasty was doomed anyway, as he was of the family of Benjamin. But David was of the family of Judah, and it was to be through his family line that God's promised descendant, through whom *all peoples on earth would be blessed* and who would have *the obedience of the nations*, would come.

Saul continued to sink into the mire of his own making when God gave him a simple instruction.

'Now go, attack the Amalekites and totally destroy everything that belongs to them. Do not spare them; put to death men and women, children and infants, cattle and sheep, camels and donkeys' (1 Sam. 15:3).

He failed to do so, keeping the best of the livestock for himself. But this was not what God had told him to do. He wanted all trace of the Amalekites destroyed. It sounds ruthless to us, and some would even question how a God of love could be so merciless. What is often overlooked is that our Father God, Ruler of the heavens and earth, is a God of righteousness as well as a God of love, and when evil rears its ugly head, particularly in these formative years of His dealings with His people, He is compelled by His very nature to take action. But to kill women, children and infants?

If we are to consider such a perceived injustice, we are forced to ask the question, were there no innocent women, children and infants in Sodom and Gomorrah when burning sulphur reigned down, or at the time of Noah's Ark, when a whole generation drowned in the waters? Of course there were – they died in the same way as the most evil and debauched of their people. Three verses force us to see the similarities and help us to understand why our kingdom of priests had to be protected from the people who surrounded it.

*'In a similar way, Sodom and Gomorrah and the surrounding
towns gave themselves up to sexual immorality and perversion.
They serve as an example of those who suffer the punishment of
eternal fire' (Jude 1:7).*

*' . . . if he did not spare the ancient world when he brought the
flood on its ungodly people, but protected Noah, a preacher of
righteousness, and seven others' (2 Pet. 2:5).*

*'And he sent you on a mission, saying, "Go and completely
destroy those wicked people, the Amalekites; make war on them
until you have wiped them out'"* (1 Sam. 15:18).

Contrast Saul with the next king of Israel, David. Here
was a ruddy young shepherd, a sensitive musician and a
mighty man of faith. How do we know this? Because he
was the only Israelite who didn't quake in his boots at the
prospect of man-to-giant combat with the nine-foot
warrior known as Goliath. Armed only with a slingshot,
he cried out:

*'You come against me with sword and spear and javelin, but I
come against you in the name of the LORD Almighty, the God of
the armies of Israel, whom you have defied. This day the LORD
will hand you over to me, and I'll strike you down and cut off
your head. Today I will give the carcasses of the Philistine army
to the birds of the air and the beasts of the earth, and the whole
world will know that there is a God in Israel. All those gathered
here will know that it is not by sword or spear that the LORD
saves; for the battle is the LORD's, and he will give all of you into
our hands' (1 Sam. 17:45–47).*

Mighty man of faith? No question about it! In contrast to
Saul, David enquired of the Lord *before* acting (except in
matters of romance, sadly) and always acknowledged that

his victories were through the hand of God, rather than his own military prowess. It was said that God gave David victory wherever he went. He was rewarded by promises from God that his descendants would be very special indeed and that his throne would be established for ever. David may not have fully understood what this meant, but it showed immense favour and grace.

King David was God's special favourite. How often we see the kingdom of his royal descendants spared judgement, for no other reason than the fact that David was their illustrious ancestor. The real reason for this was that just as God had protected David's illustrious ancestors – from Abraham, Isaac and Jacob to Boaz, Obed and Jesse – He was going to protect David's not-entirely-illustrious descendants too. This was the *Messianic* bloodline, the bloodline of the Messiah. It had been protected from the time of the Hebrews, through the Israelites' sojourn in the desert, then through the conquest of Canaan, and would pass down the generations from David for another thousand years. It may have been a royal bloodline by virtue of the fact that it would produce, in the person of Jesus of Nazareth, a Messiah king, but it managed to bypass all the hereditary kings on its journey through the ages.

Looking at the genealogy of Jesus in Luke 3, it's interesting to note that the usual suspects, Solomon and the (not so) great kings of Judah, don't get a look in. Instead we are treated to Nathan, David's ninth son, followed by a procession of unknowns, from Mattatha onwards. God has always chosen the weak, the flawed, the lowborn to accomplish His plans. It's why we feel safe in our own destiny and why we love Him so much.

The full story of how this bloodline survived the removal of the Northern Kingdom of Israel by the Assyrians and the exile and subsequent return of the

Southern Kingdom of Judah under the Babylonians is described at length in my book *Land of Many Names*.[1] It can be told in a nutshell.

King David's successor, Solomon, in common with many British middle-distance runners, had a great start but a lousy finish. First we read that God loved him at birth, which was a terrific start in life. We also read that he walked according to the statutes of his father, David, which is also encouraging. But we also read (in the same verse, in fact), '. . . *except that he offered sacrifices and burned incense on the high places*' (1 Kgs. 3:3). It was a slow, steady decline, no doubt aided by the 300 concubines that he took. The kingdom of priests was by now heavily polluted by the pagan nations and Solomon hardly helped the situation by knowingly surrounding himself with unholy influences. 1 Kings 11:4 describes it well:

> '*As Solomon grew old, his wives turned his heart after other gods, and his heart was not fully devoted to the* LORD *his God, as the heart of David his father had been.*'

The outcome of this was that the kingdom was to be split in two, Israel in the north and Judah in the south. Each was ruled by a different set of kings. Most fell far short of the standard set by King David. This was particularly so for the kings of the Northern Kingdom, who were taken into captivity by the Assyrian invaders and were never heard of again. For the Southern Kingdom of Judah it was a different story. Although the kings of Judah were not as evil as their northern counterparts, most were bad enough to invite the worst kinds of judgement from God, who has the highest standards. But they could never have met with the fate of Israel for the simple reason that it would have signalled an end to the whole story. Unhappily ever after. The Jews would have gone the way of the Hittites,

Amalekites, Amorites and All-the-other-ites. That would have meant no Jesus, no Messiah and no hope for humanity. Do you really think God would have wanted that to happen?

No, of course not. In 2 Kings 8:19 we read *'Nevertheless, for the sake of his servant David, the* LORD *was not willing to destroy Judah. He had promised to maintain a lamp for David and his descendants for ever.'* God sticks to his promises. His promise to Abraham was that all nations on earth would be blessed, and to David that his house and kingdom would endure for ever. The bloodline of the Messiah, at that time coursing through the bodies of David's descendants in the tribe of Judah, had to be protected. Nevertheless God couldn't overlook the sin of the kings of Judah, particularly that of Manasseh, a complete horror of a monarch.

> *'Manasseh led them astray, so that they did more evil than the nations the* LORD *had destroyed before the Israelites' (2 Kgs. 21:9).*

So, when the Babylonians conquered the land, the bloodline moved eastwards for seventy years. The people from Judah languished 'by the waters of Babylon' until they returned to their Promised Land at the instigation of the Persian king Cyrus.

The kingdom of priests was kept intact as a people through all these upheavals. What happened to the Jews in Babylon was an interesting story. After hundreds of years in their own land, they were now strangers in a strange land. It was a huge shock to their system, as the land they had left behind was, after all, the land promised to them as their *eternal possession* by God Himself. It was the land dominated by Solomon's awesome and magnificent temple in Jerusalem, the place where God was said to reside, the only place where sacrifices could be made. How were the Jews to worship their God now that the temple was inaccessible to them? There was only one thing for it; they had to adapt to their new situation – or die. It is important to realise that in God's eyes, the *people* of Israel have been and always will be of much greater importance than the *land* of Israel. It wasn't the land that was going to produce the Messiah; it wasn't the land that was going to bless the world. The *land* of Israel never has been and never will be a blessing, unless the *people* of Israel are living in the land. History bears this out. So our attention now moves to the *people* of Israel, exiled from the land and living in Babylon.

Now the Babylonians did not take all Jews into captivity; they took only the cream of society, leaving the dregs behind. A new community was created, adapting to the lack of a single focus by meeting in synagogues (a new concept) and *yeshivas* (places of learning). They lived along the Chebar river (the river of Babylon) and were allowed to farm and build houses for themselves. The head of the community was the *Resh Galusa*, who always had to be a direct descendant of King David. But we know that none of them formed part of the Messianic bloodline, because that privilege was held by Zerubbabel, who led the exiles back to the Promised Land at the earliest opportunity. This whole exile shouldn't have been a surprise to them. The prophet Jeremiah had already spoken of it, given the reasons for it and proclaimed when there'd be an end to it.

'This is what the LORD Almighty, the God of Israel, says to all those I carried into exile from Jerusalem to Babylon: "Build houses and settle down; plant gardens and eat what they produce. Marry and have sons and daughters; find wives for your sons and give your daughters in marriage, so that they too *may have sons and daughters. Increase in number there; do not decrease. Also, seek the peace and prosperity of the city to which I have carried you into exile. . . ." This is what the Lord says: "When seventy years are completed for Babylon, I will come to you and fulfil my gracious promise to bring you back to this place"' (Jer. 29:4–7,10).*

When their time was up in the divine calendar and God made the coast clear for a return to the Promised Land, there were up to a million Jewish exiles in Babylonia. Of these, only 42,000 returned, mainly from the tribes of Judah and Benjamin, plus a number of priests and Levites – just a few per cent, the others being happy to live out their days in exile. A similar situation exists today, with the majority of Jews living outside Israel, mainly in the USA and the western world. The Babylonian community was to become an important Jewish centre, but we are following that minority who returned to the Promised Land, following the spirit of their ancestors who understood the significance of God's promises.

They returned with Zerubbabel to help rebuild the temple in Jerusalem, the Second Temple, completed in 516 BC. More returned sixty years later with Ezra the priest, who instigated a spiritual revival among a people who were in dire need of some 'old fashioned religion'. The kingdom of priests was reminded of who they were meant to be.

But a decline set in, and very soon there were no prophets in the land to bring them back to God. God's voice was seemingly silent for around 450 years, a time that saw the rise of the Ancient Greek civilisation, bringing ideas and concepts that would prove utterly alien and an abomination to the Jewish mind. Alexander the Great conquered them in 331 BC, introducing this new way of life to the Jewish inhabitants. The process was called *Hellenisation* and was to provide a significant threat to the survival of the Jews as a distinct people. The kingdom of priests was confronted with a new enemy and battle lines were drawn.

Many Jews learnt to speak Greek and took on Greek customs. Although there was a degree of coercion, many of them didn't need to be pushed. After all, the Greek philosophy of life basically meant enjoying yourself, having a good time and prancing about naked (in sports arenas). For those who were that way inclined, it was a welcome release from two thousand years of rules and regulations, but, as we know from our modern experience, life without rules and regulations is not really a life of freedom. Many took on Greek names and frequented Greek theatres and sports events. These were Hellenised Jews and were as good as lost to the community. The others held fast to their Jewish customs, often to the point of death, upholding reverence for God and His laws.

All the time, through the whole sweep of history from Abraham onwards, God was sifting His people. As the family tree of the generations grew and widened, the line of promise, the Messianic bloodline, was following the narrower route. Many were discarded on the way – Ishmael, Esau, the Northern Kingdom, those left behind during the exile, those left in Babylon and the Jews who were assimilated into the Greek culture.

But many resisted the lure. For them the law laid down by Moses was God-given and sufficient, and surely the Messiah king would come forth soon from the illustrious line of David. It wasn't always easy to hold to these views, particularly under the reign of Antiochus IV Epiphanes. He outlawed the keeping of the Sabbath and the rite of circumcision, and many Jews, the first martyrs, died when they protested. This was a source of amazement for the Greek rulers, more used to seeing conquered people submitting to their ways. These people were actually dying for their beliefs! It was unheard of. Our kingdom of priests was living up to its name.

This assault on their religion had a unifying and positive effect for those who stayed 'within the fold'. Education was all-important. Jewish boys were educated in the *Torah* (the five books of Moses), synagogues became a strong focus for religious life and the Pharisees appeared on the scene. Though they are much maligned by many Christians, who focus on them simply as a contrast to the teachings of Jesus, it's important to note that they had been a breath of fresh air when they first appeared on the scene two hundred years earlier. It was their desire and intention that Jews should seek holiness through study of the *Torah*. More than any other group at that time, the Pharisees were truly the people's champions on spiritual matters, and by the time we reach the time of Jesus, they were the religious establishment.

Jesus of Nazareth changed everything. He was truly the fulcrum of history, especially so for the Jews, not just those living at that time in the Promised Land, but for every Jew who has ever lived. Whatever we believe about him, a study of history will show us that Jews in the Christian era have suffered untold misery, seemingly as a result of the actions of a relatively small group of Jews living in Jerusalem over the period of a single week in around AD 34.

What had happened, in the context of our developing story, is that our Messianic bloodline, edging its way through history through such giants as Abraham, Jacob and David, had reached its fulfilment. It had survived the Canaanites, Assyrians, Babylonians, Persians, Greeks and Romans. God had nurtured this precious seed, as a gardener guarding the well-being of tender young shoots. The clock ticked away as new lives drew closer to the end . . . Matthat . . . Heli . . . Mary . . . until finally it stopped: Jesus.

Of course one could write a library – and many have – about Jesus and his mission, but all we are doing in this study is to examine the effect that his life had on the Jews of his day.

A key to our understanding of this matter is to examine how the nature of the Jews' relationship with their God had changed since the Babylonian exile. Or rather, how the ways in which they managed to *anger* their God had changed.

The dominant reason for the exile was their *idolatry*, forever prostituting themselves to foreign gods, gods made of stone and fashioned by the corrupting influences of unclean spirits. Since the exile they had no longer chased after the gods of their neighbours; the gods of Persia, Greece and Rome had no appeal for them. Our kingdom of priests had been cemented together like never before, one people under one God, the God of Abraham, Isaac and Jacob. The problem was not *whom* they worshipped, but *how* they worshipped Him. They had built a hedge around the simple laws that God had given them at Sinai, adding more and more rules and regulations to convert the simple act of following God's ways from a joy to a burden. We know this as *Pharisaism*, which is a little unfair on the Pharisees, who started out as real people of revival and ended up, at the time of Jesus, no worse than many modern-day rule-laden and judgemental clergymen, who can be found lurking in the corridors of churches throughout the world. There's no doubt that if Jesus were to appear today in the flesh, many church leaders would reject him in the same way as the Pharisees of old did – it takes great faith and courage to mount a challenge to established religious systems.

Needless to say, the life and death and resurrected life of Jesus were dramatic, in different ways, for those who accepted him and for those who rejected him. The crux of the matter was that while many Jews accepted Jesus for who he claimed to be, the majority didn't, and the generation that witnessed the crucifixion was to reap the whirlwind. Jesus himself warned them of this near the end of his life.

> *'When you see Jerusalem being surrounded by armies, you will know that its desolation is near. Then let those who are in Judea flee to the mountains, let those in the city get out, and let those in the country not enter the city. For this is the time of punishment in fulfilment of all that has been written. How dreadful it will be in those days for pregnant women and nursing mothers! There will be great distress in the land and wrath against this people. They will fall by the sword and will be taken as prisoners to all the nations. Jerusalem will be trampled on by the Gentiles until the times of the Gentiles are fulfilled' (Lk. 21:20–24).*

In AD 70 the Gentile Roman army trampled on Jerusalem, killing 600,000 Jews and exiling most of the rest from the Promised Land. It is worth noting that the Jewish followers of Jesus had already left for Pella in the east by then, having heeded the words of the above prophecy.

Different explanations are given for this horrific event, depending on the perspective of the speaker. But for a Bible believer, when one considers the sins that led to the seventy-year exile to Babylon hundreds of years earlier, there must have been a *serious* dislocation between God and His kingdom of priests to warrant an exile that was to last nearly two thousand years.

We have learnt that . . .
The Jews became God's kingdom of priests, a people who would live apart from the other nations, bound together through the laws and instructions of the *Torah* and an agency for a bloodline that was to reach its fulfilment in the person of Jesus of Nazareth.

NOTES

1 *The Land of Many Names* (Authentic Media, 2002). This book examines the covenants between God and the Jewish people in the context of the land of Israel. It addresses the issue of 'Replacement Theology', looking at both the Bible and history.

Chapter 3

Galut

The Gentile world calls it *Diaspora*, although this word has been applied to any instance of large groups of people moving between nations, for whatever reason. The Jews themselves call it *Galut*, a term specific to their unique circumstances. It means 'exile', enforced removal from one's native country.

So the Jews were forcibly removed from their native country, from the Promised Land given to them by God Himself some two thousand years earlier. Who did the ejecting? On the face of it, it was the Romans, driving them into exile for being a thorn in their side, for not lying down in silence and allowing themselves to be conquered like everyone else. But the Romans themselves, just like the Assyrians, Babylonians, Persians and Greeks earlier, were mere instruments in the hand of God, who is so interested in the comings and goings of His people, Israel, that He says, in Deuteronomy 32:8:

> *'When the Most High gave the nations their inheritance, when he divided all mankind, he set up boundaries for the peoples according to the number of the sons of Israel.'*

Whatever this exactly means, it does indicate the central place occupied by 'the sons of Israel' in God's dealings with humanity. The undeniable fact is that just as He had used the Babylonians to exile the Jews from their land the first time, He was now using the Romans to exile them for a second time. And although the first exile was to last only seventy years, this second exile was to prove far more long-lasting.

Was this exile to be permanent? After all, when the people of the northern nation of Israel were led into captivity by the Assyrians, they disappeared from history – unless you truly believe they re-emerged as Red Indians, Salt Lake Mormons, Rastafarians or Prince Charles!

As outlined in the last chapter, the main purpose of the kingdom of priests was to fulfil the plans of God. A 'separated' people had to be nurtured, protected and directed so that the Messiah of humanity could appear at a point in history. Jesus of Nazareth had to come to fulfil the prophecies of the Hebrew scriptures, and for this to happen, the bloodline of David had to survive the Assyrians, the Babylonians, the Greeks and the Romans. Despite attempts by Herod the Great to kill him before he had a chance to start his ministry (Mt. 2:16), Jesus was born to a people under harsh Roman occupation, but a people intact after centuries of persecution and hardship.

So that should have been that. Jesus had arrived and now we see, just forty years after his crucifixion, his people had been sent out into exile, into *Galut*. If the Jews were now a spent force, the sensible thing for God would be to make this second exile a permanent one. Surely, some say, the Jews were now finished. The Messiah had come and most of them had rejected him, so they'd had their day and they'd blown it.

But not so. God hadn't finished with the Jews yet. Jeremiah 31:35–37 gives a reminder:

> 'This is what the LORD says, he who appoints the sun to shine by
> day, who decrees the moon and stars to shine by night, who stirs
> up the sea so that its waves roar – the LORD Almighty is his
> name: "Only if these decrees vanish from my sight," declares the
> LORD, "will the descendants of Israel ever cease to be a nation
> before me." This is what the LORD says: "Only if the heavens
> above can be measured and the foundations of the earth below be
> searched out will I reject all the descendants of Israel because of
> all they have done," declares the LORD.'

So there was still a future for the Jewish people, after their
exile from the Promised Land. But it wasn't the future
they would have chosen. It wasn't going to be an easy
ride.

Witness a typical conversation between a Jew and a
Gentile Christian:

Christian: God really loves the Jewish people, you know.
It says so in the scriptures.

Jew: And how does He show this love for us? Tell
me; I need to know.

Christian: Well, He has made sure that despite all that
the world has thrown at you for the past two
thousand years or so, you are still here. You've
survived. Isn't that proof of His love?

Jew: And *how* does that show His love for us?

Christian: Because He brought you through the troubles.
Look, you've outlived the Romans, the
Greeks, the Assyrians, the Babylonians, the
Nazis. You've triumphed over all of them.

Jew: Triumph? I see no triumph in the ghetto, in the
concentration camp. How is this triumph? We
may survive these things, but only so we can
go through a new set of troubles. Why can't
we be like other people? To be born, to be left

alone in peace and then to die of peaceful old age, just like everyone else.

Christian: But you're God's chosen people!

Jew: Chosen for what? For persecution? For hatred? As scapegoats for the world's problems? If this is what being chosen is all about, you can keep it!

It's a hard one to answer, but you can appreciate the Jewish position. If you're told of God's love for the Jewish people but then balance that against all the evil that has been directed towards these same people, you cannot help questioning whether this God is ineffectual and powerless to protect those He claims to love.

What is the nature of this love? It certainly seems to defy the usual definitions. To our eyes it's not a love of a man for his wife, protecting her from harm with strong arms, providing for her needs from the fruits of his labour. God is not seen to offer each individual Jew this kind of protection and provision; if He were, what went wrong in the Holocaust, or during the pogroms, or the suicide bombings in modern Israel?

God's love for the Jewish people is not expressed in this way. In fact individual Jews, unless they have come into a personal covenant relationship with God, are treated just like any other individual. Instead we must look at the wider picture, at the Jewish people as a whole.

God's dealings with nations are very different to His dealings with individuals. When we are told about God's love for the Jewish people it doesn't mean that an individual Jew has a higher value in His eyes than a Gentile. That would make a Gentile a second-class citizen in God's eyes and that's not how He works. A Jew has no direct route to heaven; he has to qualify for the privilege in exactly the same way as a Gentile. There's no fast track to paradise for the chosen people.

God's promises to the Jewish people are exactly what it says on the packaging – His promises to the Jewish *people*, not to the Jewish individual. God's love for the Jewish people promises not individual survival but *national* survival. This is an important fact and is key to our understanding of the whole subject.

Let's look at a few of God's promises to the Jewish people:

● God promises them a life of purpose and destiny:

> 'For you are a people holy to the LORD your God. The LORD your God has chosen you out of all the peoples on the face of the earth to be his people, his treasured possession' (Deut. 7:6).

● God assures them of His love:

> 'The LORD did not set his affection on you and choose you because you were more numerous than other peoples, for you were the fewest of all peoples. But it was because the LORD loved you and kept the oath he swore to your forefathers that he brought you out with a mighty hand and redeemed you from the land of slavery, from the power of Pharaoh king of Egypt' (Deut. 7:7–8).

> 'I have loved you with an everlasting love' (Jer. 31:3).

● God promises them a living relationship with Him:

> 'If you fully obey the LORD your God and carefully follow all his commands that I give you today, the LORD your God will set you high above all the nations on earth. All these blessings will come upon you and accompany you if you obey the LORD your God' (Deut. 28:1–2).

● God promises them national survival beyond all natural expectations:

> *'This is what the LORD says, he who appoints the sun to shine by day, who decrees the moon and stars to shine by night, who stirs up the sea so that its waves roar – the LORD Almighty is his name: "Only if these decrees vanish from my sight," declares the LORD, "will the descendants of Israel ever cease to be a nation before me"' (Jer. 31:35–36).*

This is an interesting list, particularly for a Christian, because we can see many similarities between God's package of benefits for the Jewish people and those He offers to individual Christians (both Jew and Gentile). To illustrate this, I will repeat the list, but will change the reference verses.

● God promises Christians a life of purpose and destiny:

> *'. . . and from Jesus Christ, who is the faithful witness, the firstborn from the dead, and the ruler of the kings of the earth. To him who loves us and has freed us from our sins by his blood, and has made us to be a kingdom and priests to serve his God and Father – to him be glory and power for ever and ever! Amen' (Rev. 1:5–6).*

● God assures Christians of His love:

> *'I in them and you in me. May they be brought to complete unity to let the world know that you sent me and have loved them even as you have loved me' (Jn. 17:23).*

● God promises Christians a living relationship with Him:

'If we confess our sins, he is faithful and just and will forgive us our sins and purify us from all unrighteousness' (1 Jn. 1:9).

● God promises Christians survival beyond all natural expectations (i.e. eternal life):

'For God so loved the world that he gave his one and only Son, that whoever believes in him shall not perish but have eternal life' (Jn. 3:16).

Now this is just an observation, not doctrine. No doubt a theologian could tear it to pieces on closer scrutiny. But this is not the point: it is just an illustration. The real point I am making is this: God's relationship with the Jewish people is with *the nation as a whole*, not with individual Jews. His only deep relationship with individuals is with those people – whether Jew or Gentile – who have entered a covenant with Him as Christians.

This can be further illustrated when we look at the following two verses.

First we consider the *Jewish nation* at the time of King Solomon:

'When your people Israel have been defeated by an enemy because they have sinned against you, and when they turn back to you and confess your name, praying and making supplication to you in this temple, then hear from heaven and forgive the sin of your people Israel and bring them back to the land you gave to their fathers' (1 Kgs. 8:33–34).

Then we compare it with the New Testament verse speaking about the *individual Christian*:

'If we confess our sins, he is faithful and just and will forgive us our sins and purify us from all unrighteousness' (1 Jn. 1:9).

You can see the pattern. In the Old Covenant, forgiveness and restitution tend to be applied to the Jewish nation as a whole, but in the New Covenant it is with individuals, Jew and Gentile, who have entered a personal relationship with God.

A major point, and one often misunderstood by Christians, is that God does not treat *individual* Jews any differently from individual Gentiles. For them personally to know a life of purpose and destiny, a life everlasting and a life filled with love from their Creator, they have to follow the same rules as Gentiles – a personal relationship with the risen Jesus. Jews who have become believers in Jesus are already twice blessed, on account of their personal relationship with God and on account of the national covenant relationship between God and *all* Jewish people (whether they know it or not).

But history shows us that this relationship between God and the Jewish people does not come without cost. Where there are privileges there are responsibilities, even when the privileges are not accepted.

It will help us to understand this if we return to our historical journey. It is AD 130.

Jerusalem was in ruins. Roman vengeance was thorough and devastating. A story is told of Rabbi Akiva, the spiritual giant of his day.[1] One day he travelled to the ruined city with four other rabbis and, when they arrived, the desolate sight that greeted them filled them with such sorrow that they all rent their garments and mourned. As they approached the site of the ruined temple they saw a fox prowling through what was left of the Holy of Holies. At this sight his four companions wept, but Rabbi Akiva was filled with joy.

'*Why are you so happy?*' they exclaimed.

'*Why do you weep?*' was his reply.

'In the holiest of all places, where once only the High Priest was permitted, foxes now roam. Isn't that enough to make you weep?' they replied.

'And for that very same reason I am joyful,' said Rabbi Akiva. 'In the Book of Micah it says "Jerusalem will become a heap of rubble, the temple hill a mound overgrown with thickets." In the Book of Zechariah it says, "Once again men and women of ripe old age will sit in the streets of Jerusalem, each with cane in hand because of his age." Until the first prophecy came to pass, I may have doubted the truth of the second. Now that the first prophecy has been fulfilled, I can have no doubt at all that the second will also, one day, come true!'

There's something about this story that speaks volumes about the Jewish spirit and perhaps gives us a key to understanding how God's kingdom of priests was going to survive in the *Galut*.

And what a terrible time they had. There are two major characteristics of the *Galut* that make it unique. Firstly, the amazing distances to which Jews were dispersed and the contributions they made to the places where they found themselves. Secondly, the hatred they found in virtually every community.

To illustrate these facts, let's take a whistle-stop tour through time and space:[2]

Central Asia:	Heathen Khazars converted to Judaism in AD 700.
Isfahan (Persia):	Jews forbidden to build houses as high as those of their Muslim neighbours.
Capua (Italy):	Jewish director of mint, 1000.
Bulgaria:	Jewish slave-trading with Christians in 1096.
Peking (China):	Small Jewish trading community here by 1200.

Exeter (England):	Synod forbids Jews to hold public office, 1281.
Toledo (Spain):	Twelve thousand Jews massacred by mob, 1355.
Strasbourg (France):	No Jew allowed in city between 1388 and 1767.
Goa (India):	More than one hundred Jews burned by Inquisition.
Moscow (Russia):	Jewish court physician killed for failing to cure nobleman, 1490.
Cracow (Poland):	Jews forced into ghetto, 1494.
Heidelberg (Germany):	Jew helped finance Austrian wars against Turkey, 1680.
Buenos Aires (Argentina):	More than four thousand Jews living in city, 1754.
Green Bay (USA):	Jew opens trading post with Indians, 1794.
Leipzig (Germany):	Jews in Prussian Army against Napoleon, 1813.
St Petersburg (Russia):	Burning and banning of Jewish books, 1837.
Meshed (Persia):	All Jews forcibly converted to Islam, 1838.
Suez (Egypt):	Jew loans money to Britain to buy Suez Canal, 1876.
Ekron (Palestine):	Bought by German Jew for South Russian Jews, 1884.
Baku (Azerbaijan):	Thirty thousand 'Mountain Jews' with own language, 1900.
Recife (Brazil):	One thousand Jews establish colony, 1904.
Vietnam:	Ho Chi Minh offers Jews home in exile, 1946.

Good and bad, but mostly bad. The *Galut* was certainly thorough in its scope and severity. We can see distinct Jewish communities all over the world at different times. Mostly they are on the move, particularly in places where, tragically, their presence had been an offence to the 'Christian' church. Expelled from England, France, Spain, Germany and Portugal at various times and always living in a climate of fear and uncertainty, they surely didn't have a life fitting for a kingdom of priests.

Then, against all odds, expectations and human reason, it began to reverse itself. Jews, who had been wandering the nations for centuries, began to return home to the Promised Land. What started as a trickle became a torrent, leading to the formation of the nation of Israel in 1948. There was no historical precedent for this; it was something new. God was doing something amazing, yet Bible believers should not be surprised, as He had spoken of it enough times well in advance in His scriptures.

In order to appreciate the effect of the *Galut* we will concentrate on a microcosm of the whole experience, with a geographical snapshot of the Jewish experience in just one place, London,[3] to see what we can learn.

The crowning of Richard the Lionheart at Westminster was a time of great rejoicing for the people, but not for all of them. The Jews of the country had only been around since 1066, when they came over from France with William the Conqueror, as bankers and financial consultants. But they were always under suspicion, an attitude hardly discouraged by the church, and this situation came to a head at the coronation. The Jews arrived at Westminster bearing gifts, but were refused entry and pelted by mobs incited by rumours that the king wanted them exterminated. Riots ensued, resulting in the death of 30 Jews and the burning of many Jewish homes. This act was to be repeated all over the country; in York, for example, Jews committed suicide rather than be killed by a bloodthirsty mob. Their crime? Just being Jews.

A hundred years later the situation had reached the point of no return, particularly as the Italians had been lined up to take over the financial affairs of the kingdom. There was now no more need for Jewish expertise and the king's protection was removed. The result was full-blown persecution of the Jews, who were blamed for every calamity going. In 1287, Edward I imprisoned 3,000 of them on a charge of doctoring the coinage and held them to ransom. The ransom was paid, but in 1290 it was decided to expel all Jews from England. By November 1, thousands had fled, mostly to France. They had to pay their own passage and were allowed to take only what they could carry. Some of them were robbed and cast overboard by the ships' captains during the voyage. England was the first country to kick out the Jews, and it was to be an exile that lasted 366 years.

Oliver Cromwell was growing old and well established as the Lord Protector of England when he felt empowered to invite the Jews back. Although he was deeply religious and positively inclined towards the Jews on account of the Puritan partiality for the Old Testament, it was the politician in him that was the key factor. It was a time of alliances among the European nations, and it was important to know what your enemy was up to. Who better to have on your side than the Jews, true internationalists, with their interests in Spanish and Portuguese trade and influences stretching from Germany to the Dutch East Indies? Who better to bring trade to the country and also to act as spies on his behalf?

In 1655 he summoned the Dutch Rabbi Manasseh ben Israel to plead the case for the readmission of Jews to England. He did so in a document called the *Humble Address*, in which he felt it necessary to address the three major accusations made by Christians against the Jews back in the days when they were living in England. Firstly, the question of usury, the charging of excessive interest on loans. He insisted that the rate of interest they charged was the same as that charged by Christian moneylenders and that their religion had always forbidden them to do otherwise. Secondly, he insisted in the strongest terms that Jews did *not* kill Christian children to make *Matzoh* bread for Passover. Thirdly, that Jews did *not* actively proselytise and were *not* in the business of enticing innocent Christians into Judaism.

This was OK for Cromwell, but not for many of his advisors, who were still holding onto the old prejudices. A committee met in the Council Chamber at Whitehall that December. It consisted of representatives of the army, the law and the trading interests, and 16 Christian leaders, the majority of whom Cromwell had carefully selected on account of their supposed approval of religious toleration. The only thing they really agreed on was that the 1290 expulsion of the Jews had been illegal, but they were unwilling to act on this realisation. So Cromwell convened another meeting with a few extra delegates who he thought would be more favourable towards the Jews. But the outcome was the same and an air of hostility had soured the proceedings.

So Cromwell played the religious card, saying that as the Bible speaks of their conversion, they need to be in a place where the Gospel is being preached, namely England! He then mocked this assembly, accusing them of cowardice and of being afraid that the Jewish merchants would take away their livelihood.

But it was for nothing, so he vacated the chair and closed the conference. Now it was up to the God of history to intervene.

It was an open secret that there were some Jews already

in England. These were the secret Jews, the *Marranos* (literally 'pigs'), Spanish and Portuguese Jews who, as a result of the Inquisition, had 'converted' to Christianity but continued to practise their Judaism in secret. Forty *Marrano* families had settled in England and one of their number, Roderigo Lopez, had even become a medical attendant to Elizabeth II in 1586.

After the conference had broken down, war broke out with Spain, and the Spanish *Marranos* were unable to live in England as Spanish citizens. So in 1656, relying upon the decision that the expulsion of 1290 was no longer valid, they openly threw off their disguise and assumed the position of Jews. Cromwell agreed to this, particularly after a petition was made to him by Manasseh ben Israel and six other prominent Jews, asking whether they might meet openly without fear of molestation and bury their dead in peace.

Interestingly, there is no recorded answer to this petition, as the relevant Council minutes have never been found. What is certain, however, is that they were subsequently confident enough to rent a house for use as a synagogue, and Jews began to trickle back into England for the first time in nearly four hundred years.

History shows us that the Jews who were taken in by England in the seventeenth century, and thus protected from the hatred shown towards them in Europe, were to flourish in their new country, becoming bankers and statesmen, even producing a prime minister and confidants to royalty, thus playing a major part in the growth of the British Empire at the expense of those countries they had left behind.

These Jews who trickled into England from 1656 onwards were Spanish and Portuguese, *Sephardi* Jews, who had fled their native lands because of the persecutions initiated by the Inquisition but had found temporary refuge in Holland, where they made a huge contribution to the golden age of Dutch commercial enterprise and helped make Amsterdam the richest city in the world at that time.

The site of the first synagogue in England for these *Sephardi* Jews is commemorated by a blue plaque in Creechurch Lane, on the eastern fringes of the City of London. One day in 1662 Samuel Pepys, the great diarist, paid them a visit and was greatly perturbed by their exuberance.[4]

> *'. . . But, Lord! To see the disorder, laughing, sporting, and no attention, but confusion in all their service, more like brutes than people knowing the true God . . . I never did see so much, or could have imagined there had been any religion in the whole world so absurdly performed as this.'*

In fact he had stumbled on a celebration of *Simchat Torah*, a festival known for its exuberance, and one would expect a similar reaction if a present-day orthodox Jew had witnessed a modern charismatic Christian worship service!

Very soon the congregation had grown too large for the synagogue, and a new one was built in 1701. This was Bevis Marks synagogue, built within the City walls and still functioning today as the oldest synagogue in England. In fact some of the benches there in current use actually pre-date the original synagogue and are said to be the largest collection of Cromwellian benches in the world. Ladino, a form of Spanish spoken by fifteenth-century Jews expelled from Spain to Turkey, is also still used in the services. The architect, Joseph Avis, was a Quaker and it is said that he refused to make a profit from building a house of God and returned all profits to the congregation.

This was not the whole story, because there were also other Jews making their way over from Holland. These were the *Ashkenazi* Jews – of Dutch, Polish and German descent. They intended to build a synagogue and there was even talk that St Paul's Cathedral, recently rebuilt after the Great Fire of London, would be offered to the Jews, but sufficient funds couldn't be raised. So they built their own synagogue, the Great Synagogue at Duke's Place, just along the wall from Bevis Marks. This place remained until the Second World War, when it became another victim of the Nazi war effort.

So the Jews settled and prospered, building their synagogues and mainly living close to them. More synagogues were built in the following years and the Jewish community began to spread out through the region as a whole. In 1795 it was estimated that there were around 25,000 Jews in England, with around 75 per cent of these in London.

This was the third and largest wave of Jewish immigration to these shores. The first to arrive, numbered in their hundreds, were the financiers accompanying the Norman conquest. The second, in their thousands, following the initiative of Oliver Cromwell, were from Holland and Germany, a people forever on the move around Europe. The third, numbered in the tens of thousands, came between 1880 and 1905, fleeing from persecution in the lands to the east, mainly Russia and Poland.

Jewish immigration to the area came to a full stop when, after much pressure from the indigenous population (namely the anti-Semitic *British Brothers League*), parliament passed the Aliens Act in 1905, refusing entry to Britain to *undesirable aliens*. This of course meant Jews from the east, and reduced immigration by 40 per cent. Nevertheless, in the period since 1881, over 100,000 Jews had found refuge in Whitechapel and Spitalfields. A grateful Jewish population commemorated this fact by tossing their pennies into a large coffer and having a monument built to King Edward VII in 1911. This still stands opposite London Hospital, outside the McDonald's and between the Bangladeshi market stalls.

Now there are fewer than 300,000 Jews in the UK, a number dwindling by the year, mainly because of assimilation. Despite the subtle growth of anti-Semitism, Jews in the UK feel fairly settled. But then again, so did Jews in Germany in the 1930s, just before the Nazi holocaust. In July 2004, Ariel Sharon, the Israeli Prime Minister, called on French Jews to move to Israel 'immediately', because of the worrying rise of anti-Jewish feeling in France. Only time will tell if the *Galut* will end with a whimper or a bang.

Finally, it is time to ask the big question. How does the *Galut* fit in with the message of the Bible? Why would God allow this to happen to our children of promise, our kingdom of priests? A big question that needs an answer. Moses offers some clues in the Book of Deuteronomy:

'Just as it pleased the LORD *to make you prosper and increase in number, so it will please him to ruin and destroy you. You will be uprooted from the land you are entering to possess. Then the* LORD *will scatter you among all nations, from one end of the earth to the other. There you will worship other gods – gods of wood and stone, which neither you nor your fathers have known. Among those nations you will find no repose, no resting place for the sole of your foot. There the* LORD *will give you an anxious mind, eyes weary with longing, and a despairing heart. You will live in constant suspense, filled with dread both night and day, never sure of your life. In the morning you will say, "If only it were evening!" and in the evening, "If only it were morning!" – because of the terror that will fill your hearts and the sights that*

your eyes will see' (Deut. 28:63–67).

These words, written over 3,500 years ago, send a chill down the spine when we consider the *Galut*. What could the Jewish people have done to deserve such a judgement? Could this all have been a result of the life of one man, Jesus of Nazareth, Jesus the Messiah? In the next chapter we discuss this further.

We have learnt that . . .
The Jews have suffered an exile, the *Galut*, unique in that although they were dispersed to virtually every country in the world, they have survived as a distinct people and, after 2,000 years, have started to return to their point of origin.

NOTES

1 From *Midrash Rabba Eicha*, 5.
2 These facts are mainly taken from *The Jewish History Atlas*, Martin Gilbert.
3 The Jewish experience in London is such a fascinating subject for me that I occasionally conduct historical walking tours of the Jewish East End of London. More information is at www.londonjewishtours.com
4 *Diary of Samuel Pepys*, 14 October 1662.

Chapter 4

'Christ Killers'

A small news item caught my eye as I was researching this book. It concerned the current Bishop of Durham's reaction to a small addition to the Church of England's prayer book at Easter-time.[1] The prayer in question was written as God speaking to His church, saying, *'I grafted you into the tree of my chosen Israel and you turned on them with persecution and mass murder. I made you joint heirs with them of my covenants, but you made them scapegoats for your own guilt.'*

'This is turning the church into a scapegoat for anti-Semitism,' he said, adding that he interpreted the prayer as God accusing the Christians of persecution and of inducing an anti-Semitic culling of the Jews. He said that this prayer made several statements that were *'biblically and theologically unjustifiable'* and also remarked that the thrust of the prayer had *'never been mainstream Church of England teaching.'*

Perhaps he's right. Perhaps the sentiments of the prayer are going a little too far and it's all a bit unfair on our state church. Words mean nothing unless backed with facts, so we must explore these facts ourselves to see whether the Bishop of Durham is justified in his righteous anger.

In the previous chapter we met Rabbi Akiva, who felt real joy and certainty that, just as it said in the Book of Zechariah, one day in the future there would be peace in Jerusalem. He was a man of great faith and was willing to stand up and be counted when it mattered. He was the latest in a long line of Jewish martyrs, who died performing *Kiddush HaShem*, the highest calling for any Jew. He was tortured and killed by the Romans and it is said that he suffered no pain until the red-hot iron combs they were using to peel the skin from his flesh reached the place on his forehead where his *tefillin* would rest, and it was then that he screamed, *'Shema Yisrael, Adonai Elohaynu, Adonai, Echad.'* (*'Hear, O Israel: the Lord our God, the Lord is one'*) (Deut. 6:4).

Kiddush HaShem, Sanctification of the Name, is to give up one's life rather than submit to the betrayal of one's belief in God and abandonment of Judaism for another religion. Akiva died a martyr, a tradition of the Jews way before the Christians came along. It is a sad and tragic fact that *Kiddush HaShem* has resulted more from Christian persecution than from any other. How on earth can that be?

If *anti-Semitism* is defined as hatred of the Jews, how would we define *Christian anti-Semitism*? That's surely an oxymoron, two words that couldn't possibly inhabit the same sentence, let alone be joined together as a phrase. That's true, which is why we'll be using instead the phrase 'Christian' anti-Semitism. A subtle change, but a necessary one because there is absolutely, definitely nothing *Christian* about anti-Semitism, yet more anti-Semitic acts have been committed by 'Christians' than by any other group of people. Witness the following.

On 15 July 1099, the warriors of the First Crusade arrived in Jerusalem and proceeded to slaughter every Jew they could find, burning many alive in the synagogue. After this monstrous act they went on a procession to church, singing hymns on the way and wading ankle deep in the blood of their victims. Tens of thousands of Jews and Muslims were massacred at the hands of the 'Christians'. An eyewitness, William, Archbishop of Tyre, said, *'They cut down with the sword every one whom they found in Jerusalem, and spared no one. The victors were covered with blood from head to foot. It was a most affecting sight which filled the heart with holy joy to see the people tread the holy places in the fervour of an excellent devotion.'*[2]

Needless to say, *Kiddush HaShem* became commonplace during the Crusades. The Crusaders created the first instance of large numbers of Jews dying for *Kiddush HaShem*. Thousands of Jewish women, fearing rape, chose to die for *Kiddush HaShem*. They died as martyrs to the very same God that their persecutors claimed to worship. It was an unbelievable tragedy and, human sensibilities aside, can you imagine what this did to the heart of God? Is it not surprising that Jews through the ages, witnessing these and other acts perpetrated by 'Christians', have said, *'If this is Christianity then you can keep it!'* We must turn the remark into a question and ask, *'Is this Christianity and, if so, what went wrong? Because it's surely not the faith in a risen Jesus Christ.'* So what went wrong?

What went wrong was that the early Gentile church made a decision, based on a questionable interpretation of the Bible, that the Jews were no longer God's chosen people and certainly not a kingdom of priests. They took it further by declaring that not only had the Jews lost their privileged position, they were also eternally cursed by a fickle God, for whom love had now turned to hate. Now this was not the God who had said, *'I have loved you with an everlasting love'* (Jer. 31:3), it was not the God of the Bible, but it was a convenient 'man-made' God of the 'Christians', who were looking for justifications for their acts of hatred, greed and depravity.[3]

Mindful of the fact that these early 'Christians' had little love for their Jewish neighbours, we will now examine how their prejudices led to actions against the Jews of their day. We have to live with the shame that more acts of anti-Semitism have been committed in the name of Christianity than of any other cause in history. It is one of the greatest ironies of history that a faith based on the life and death of a Jew and spread first by fellow Jews should prove to be by far the most vicious persecutor of the Jewish race. And all in the name of its Jewish founder! So how did it start? When did our 'kingdom of priests' become 'Christ killers'?

Once the church had moved away from its Jewish origins, the church Fathers were keen to show the world how the favours of God had moved from the old flesh-and-blood natural Israel to the spanking new 'spiritual Israel', the church. They reasoned that the Jews had had their chance, and failed. *'Didn't they bring it on themselves?'* they argued. *'For surely they not only rejected Jesus, their Messiah, but they killed him as well.'*

After the death of the generation that witnessed Jesus in the flesh, the leaders of the church were Gentile and were spread throughout the Middle East and Eastern Europe. They were eager to carry out the policy, dictated by their theologians, of purging everything *Jewish* from the church. The Sabbath was a heaven-sent (excuse the pun) opportunity. The Sabbath day was too Jewish, and it was decided to change the day of rest and worship to the Sunday, the Lord's Day, the day of Jesus' resurrection. Despite the fact that God didn't have a say in the matter (and would probably have preferred that His day off and that of His followers coincided!) and that Sunday was a pagan Roman day of sun-worship, it was the first step away from the roots and towards the pagan community in which they lived. This, and the later adoption of 25

December (the Roman day of Saturnalia, a day of orgy and revelry) as Christmas Day, and Easter (a pagan fertility festival), went totally against the teaching of their leader Jesus, who told them to *'be in the world, but not of the world'*.

By the fourth century AD, Jews were being pushed to the edges of society. Laws were passed, starting with those by the Emperor Constantine that were designed to keep a safe distance between Jew and Christian. Intermarriage was expressly forbidden and was to be treated as adultery. Further laws were passed prohibiting Jews from holding high positions in government or from acting as witnesses against Christians. Needless to say, it was the death penalty for any Christian converting to Judaism.

In the Christian world, Jews found themselves driven towards one profession – the world of finance. Christian society at that time was characterised by the feudal system, with the nobles, who did the fighting, the priests, who did the praying, and the serfs, who did the work! There was a vacancy for a 'middle class', for merchants, traders and moneylenders, and the Jews fitted the bill perfectly. It was ironic that the feudal system, which stifled so many in its all-embracing grip, gave such freedom of movement to the Jews.

Moneylending became the profession that most characterised the Jews at that time and it was all because of their own book, the Bible. You see, Christians felt that the Bible forbade them to lend money to each other with interest, yet there was a growing need for credit in the expanding markets of the day, so someone had to lend the money and take the risks. Enter the Jews.

For some reason the church paid special attention to the fifth book of the *Torah*, concerning moneylending.

'Do not charge your brother interest, whether on money or food

> *or anything else that may earn interest. You may charge a*
> *foreigner interest, but not a brother Israelite, so that the Lord*
> *your God may bless you in everything you put your hand to in*
> *the land you are entering to possess' (Deut. 23:19–20).*

Suddenly the Christians were Israelites, already! Ignoring the large bulk of the 613 laws that made up the *Torah*, they focused on this one, reasoning that as they were now Israelites, that made them *foreigners* to the former Israelites – the Jews. So it was OK for Jews to lend money to Christians, who knew very well that, when push came to shove, they could always refuse to repay the loans, as the Jews were not exactly in a position to enforce any agreements made!

An example of their precarious existence was an edict by Henry III of England in 1253. In it he decreed that *'no Jew [might] remain in England unless he do the king service, and that from the hour of birth every Jew, whether male or female, [must] serve us in some way'*.[4] The same edict severely limited everyday Jewish life. Identifying badges had to be worn in public and Jews could no longer live in towns unless granted special licences by the king. Nor, in the future, could they eat or buy meat during the Lenten season. Henry also ordered that Jews worshipping in their synagogues had to *'subdue their voices in performing their ritual offices, that Christians may not hear them'*.

But there was worse, far worse. Although the popes of the day tended to protect the Jews, the church in general was no friend of the Jew. One reason was fear. Having labelled the Jews as children of the devil, the church regarded their very survival as affront, implying that the devil was gaining ground in the 'war against the saints'. Why didn't God just destroy them, to show His power? Well, He was committed to their survival, not their annihilation, and it's now clear, as we look back with hindsight, on whose side the devil was in this particular conflict. While the Jewish 'idolaters' were quietly studying the Word of God in drab *yeshivas* in Palestine and Jewish academic centres in the *Galut*, 'Christians' were either arguing among themselves and corrupting themselves and their religion with the most unbiblical practices from the pagan world, or they were being kept in ignorance of the true Word of God by the church.

Reading and writing were just for those being groomed in the church. The vast majority of citizens had never read a Bible for themselves in their life – indeed no Bibles were available in the language of the common man anyway. So all theology and expressions of Christianity came from whatever the church of the day wanted them to believe, for purposes that were more about power and greed than a desire to educate people in the liberating teachings of the Bible.

During the 'Dark Ages' – the period from the fifth to the twelfth century – the light of God's revelation through His Word, the Bible, was well and truly dimmed, except in isolated monastic communities. It was a time when 'Christianity' ruled and the reason for its darkness was that Christianity is not a religion of rule and conquest, so what actually ruled was a corruption of Jesus' teachings. Do you not think that if this really was a society ruled by the teachings of Jesus, it would have been the 'Light Ages', a period of peace, learning and tolerance? It was the complete opposite! All kinds of strange teachings, littered with superstitions and paganism, filtered to the people from the established church, and much of it concerned the Jews, the hated 'Christ killers'. Here are some of the worst examples.

The Jews were accused of causing the Black Death, the plague that swept through Europe, killing over half the population in the mid-fourteenth century. Apparently they did so by poisoning wells. The 'justification' for this accusation is that fewer Jews died from this plague than 'Christians', although the real reason was that the Jews were simply following the sensible health and sanitation guidelines in the Bible and other Jewish writings, which the 'Christians' couldn't possibly do, as the few of them who could actually read would have been quite unfamiliar with the Bible. These accusations resulted in about 350 separate massacres of Jews during the plague years, with well over 20,000 murdered.

It gets worse with an accusation born of sheer hatred and sustained by blind ignorance. It was the *blood-libels*. Jews were again and again accused of murdering Christian children and using their blood to make Passover *Matzoh* bread. These accusations were usually at Easter-time and were often accompanied by massacres of Jewish populations. The first such accusation was in 1144 in Norwich. There, Jews were charged with kidnapping a Christian child, tying him to a cross, killing him and then draining his body of blood. The baby was canonised as St William of Norwich – no doubt his short life had been extremely virtuous.

'Christian' Europe followed this lead. In 1171, 38 Jews in France were burned to death on the (false) charge of throwing a Christian child into a river. In 1255, 18 Jews were tortured and hanged in England for allegedly murdering an 8-year-old boy and using his blood for religious rites. In 1285, 180 Jews were burned in Munich, purely on the basis of a rumour that they had bled a child to death in the synagogue. In 1475, at Trent, Italy, almost all the Jews of the city were tortured and burned after a rumour started to spread that they had murdered a boy named Simon.

The irony of these accusations is that Jews to this day are prohibited by Jewish law from consuming any blood whatsoever, yet by the fourteenth century the church had adopted the doctrine of *transubstantiation*, which says that when the priest says mass (Holy Communion), the wafer and wine mystically change into the body and blood of Jesus. In effect, Christians were drinking the blood and eating the flesh of Jesus himself, according to their beliefs.

Having concocted this doctrine, they then exercised their imaginations to find new ways of persecuting Jews and came up with an extreme nastiness. It was called *host-nailing* or *the desecration of the host*. A rumour spread that once the Jews found out that the wafer (host) became the actual 'body of Christ', they began stealing the wafers and driving nails into them, so as to crucify Jesus again and again. They were also accused of trampling on the host and even urinating on it. Medieval documents tell stories describing how a Jew (usually called Abraham) would steal a wafer from a church and stick a knife in it, upon which blood would start pouring out. He would then cut it up into pieces and send it to different Jews who would continue to torture it.

To you and me it all seems like a sick joke, but to the Jews of the day it meant further slaughter. It started in 1243, when Jews were burned at the stake in Belitz, Germany, for host-nailing. Then, in Nuremberg, in 1298, 628 Jews were killed for the same offence. In 1370, in Brussels, hundreds of Jews were tortured and mutilated on the same pretext.

In 1095, Pope Urban II called for Christians throughout western Europe to travel to the 'Holy Land' to rescue the holy places from the Muslims. The result was the First Crusade, the first of eight expeditions that sent thousands of innocent people to an early grave, but achieved little for their organisers and did nothing for the cause of the Gospel of Jesus Christ.

You have already read what these Crusaders did to the Jews (and Muslims) of Jerusalem, but this was just a climax to a bloody and cursed expedition. They felt that it was their sacred duty to kill some 'Christ killers' before they departed for the holy land, so Peter the Hermit and his untrained peasant army killed hundreds of Jews in the Rhineland before leaving for the First Crusade. At about the same time, another Crusader, Count Emich of Leiningen, systematically attacked the Jewish communities in the German cities. On 3 May 1096, French and German Crusaders massacred the Jews of Speyer, in the Rhineland. In Worms, Jews hiding from the Crusaders in the Bishop's palace were mercilessly hunted and eventually committed suicide (*Kiddush HaShem*) rather than be put to death by the 'Christians'. Near Mainz, 1,014 Jews, including children, were slaughtered.

Emich believed that slaughtering the infidels who lived among Christians was a primary religious duty. He gave the Jews two options: baptism or death. While some submitted to baptism, most Jews chose *Kiddush HaShem*. Emich and his men killed thousands of Jewish men, women and children, and all traces of Jewish culture in these cities, the synagogues, the *Torah* and the *Talmud* scrolls, were completely destroyed.

The outcome was that at least ten thousand Jews out of an estimated population of about twenty to thirty thousand were murdered in 1096 as the First Crusade got underway.

European nations in turn decided that the best way to deal with the 'Jewish problem' was to get rid of them and let someone else deal with them. So during these years Jews found themselves ping-ponged across Europe. They were expelled from England in 1290, from France in 1306, from Germany in the 1350s, from Spain in 1492, from Portugal in 1496 and from the Papal States in 1569. As a result of these mass expulsions, the centre of Jewish life shifted from western Europe and Germany to Turkey and then to Poland and Russia.

But where they were needed, Jews were tolerated. Living as they did at the margins of society, Jews performed economic functions that were vital to trade and commerce. Where they were permitted to participate in the larger society, Jews thrived. During the Middle Ages in Spain, before their expulsion in 1492, Jewish philosophers, physicians, poets and writers were among the leaders of a rich cultural and intellectual life shared with Muslims and Christians.

For centuries, individual Christians and Jews had engaged in debate over the truths and merits of their respective religions. The more or less amiable tenor and informal setting of these encounters changed in 1239 when church leaders began staging public 'disputations'. Taking place before large audiences, often with kings and popes in attendance, they featured Jewish scholars forced to defend Judaism's holy books against claims made by Christians. Many of the Catholic debaters – supposedly well versed in *Torah* and *Talmud* – were converted Jews. Moreover, the Christian establishment set the ground rules: by definition, Christian theology would always be upheld as the ultimate revealed truth.

On 7 January 1413, the apostate Jew known as Geronimo de Santa Fe challenged leading Jewish scholars in Spain to disprove that specific biblical and Talmudic passages pointed to Jesus as the true Messiah. Outside the church where the 'debate' took place, frenzied mobs demonstrated their hatred of Jews, the people they believed had murdered Jesus. Inside, the Jewish debaters attempted to point out how Geronimo had misinterpreted the cited passages, but church officials frequently silenced them. As in all forced debates, the Tortosa Disputation's outcome was never in doubt: Judaism's defenders could never be declared the victors.

As an option to death or banishment, a Jew could always 'convert' to Christianity. Unlike in the early church, when the transition was relatively painless and straightforward, in fifteenth-century Spain it was a different story. These converts were known as *Conversos* or *Marranos* ('swine'). It didn't really matter how deep their new Christian convictions were, they were still hated on account of their racial origins. Here are examples of the formal declarations these *Marranos* had to make:

> 'I do here and now renounce every rite and observance of the Jewish religion, detesting all its most solemn ceremonies and tenets that in former days I kept and held. . . . I renounce the whole worship of the Hebrews, circumcision, all its legalisms, unleavened bread, Passover, the sacrificing of lambs, the feast of Weeks, Jubilees, Trumpets, Atonement, Tabernacles, and all other Hebrew feasts, their sacrifices, prayers. . . . In one word, I renounce absolutely everything Jewish.'[5]

'No one escapes the Spanish Inquisition' was the catchphrase of a particularly surreal *Monty Python* sketch on television. This was no joke, because no one did escape the Spanish Inquisition; no one escaped from the Grand Inquisitor, Tomas de Torquemada.

Set up to stamp out 'heresies' in general, the Inquisition came down heavily, not so much on the Jewish population in general, but on the *Marranos*, the Jewish Christians. It was said that *'the Devil never devised a more effective instrument of Jewish scorn and hatred of the name of Christ than the Inquisition.'*

The mildest penalty imposed on *Marranos* was the seizure of their property, followed by the public humiliation of being paraded through the streets wearing a yellow shirt emblazoned with crosses that came only to the waist, leaving the lower body uncovered. They were then flogged at the church door. A sliding scale of punishments continued up to burning at the stake, performed as a public spectacle called an *auto-da-fé* ('act of faith'). If the condemned recanted and kissed the cross, they were mercifully strangled before the fire was set. If they recanted they were burned with a quick-burning seasoned wood, but if they refused to kiss the cross they were burned with slow-burning green wood.

In 1490 there was a show-trial, the LaGuardia trial. This involved 8 Jews and *Marranos* accused of having crucified a Christian child. No victim was ever identified and no body was ever found, yet all 8 were convicted on the strength of their confessions, which were obtained through torture. They were burned at the stake.

So, given the unspeakable historical track record of the church in the treatment of Jews, it is no wonder that the Jewish people, on the whole, reject Christianity unreservedly. Yet the actions of these 'Christians' had little or nothing to do with the words of Jesus. In looking at their motives one must consider such things as pride, hate, jealousy, greed, ignorance and just about every other base emotion known to human beings. But above all, it is the curse of the anti-Semitism virus, whatever its cause, that has infected the hearts and minds of people, encouraging them in their actions, just as a cold virus inevitably produces sore throats and runny noses.

But wait, I can hear the sound of hoof-beats in the distance. Is it the cavalry, coming to rescue the Jews from the madness that surrounds them? The world is changing. A new movement, the *Reformation*, sweeps through Europe, promising liberation from the ignorance and tyranny of the Catholic Church. The key figure in this movement is Martin Luther, the founder of the Lutheran Church.

Luther makes a bold proclamation. *'Let's start reading our Bibles,'* he says. (The cavalry approaches nearer, salvation is surely close at hand?) He reads his Bible and discovers that Jesus was Jewish. He writes a pamphlet, *That Jesus Christ was born a Jew* (1523), which affirms the Jewish descent of Jesus. (The horses are so close now . . .) He denounces the wickedness of popes and priests in their attitude to Jews (even closer, I can see the whites of their eyes . . .) He advocates a loving attitude to them, to win them to Christianity. But . . .

Twenty years later he was near the end of his life. He'd achieved much, founded a church, helped to start a major religious movement.

But very few Jews had converted to Christianity!

Martin Luther's love turned to hate. He changed his attitude towards Jews (the cavalry has long since disbanded and gone home). He became hostile to them and issued a new set of pamphlets, one of them entitled *On the Jews and their Lies* (1543). In these writings we can read words he used to refer to these people he once described so favourably: *'venomous . . . thieves . . . disgusting vermin . . . a pestilence and misfortune for our country . . . children of the Devil.'*

He proposed the following remedies:

1 Set fire to their synagogues.
2 Destroy their homes.
3 Deprive them of their sacred books.
4 Withdraw their passports and travelling privileges.
5 Stop them moneylending (although it was the only 'acceptable' trade for them).
6 Give them hard physical labour.
7 Forbid rabbis to teach.

His conclusion was this: *'To sum up, dear princes and nobles who have Jews in your domains, if this advice of mine does not suit you, then find a better one so that you may all be free of this insufferable devilish burden – the Jews.'*[6]

'Find a better one?'

These were prophetic words indeed, particularly when we consider the legacy of this German preacher. In *Mein Kampf*, a book that needs no introduction, we read that Luther was one of Hitler's heroes. These words were finally renounced by the Evangelical Lutheran Church in America, but not until 1994.

As the Protestant reformation took hold, the position of Jews in Europe was unchanged. They remained subject to occasional massacres, such as those that occurred during wars between Eastern Orthodox Ukrainians and Roman Catholic Poles in the mid-seventeenth century, which rivalled the worst massacres of Jews in the Middle Ages. Periodic persecutions of Jews continued until the late eighteenth century, as history moved into the 'Age of Reason', when the church's hold on the people of Europe was loosened. Yet anti-Semitism continued in a different form. As reason took over from faith, Jews were blamed not so much as 'Christ killers' as for Christianity itself and, ironically, the injustices and cruelty committed by followers of 'religion'. Some of the most prominent figures, including Voltaire, ridiculed the Jews as a group alienated from society who practised a primitive and superstitious religion.

Until the French Revolution of 1789, Jews in Europe were viewed as outsiders with few civil rights. They were taxed as a community, not as individuals, and were forced to continue to rely on their own communities, which were strengthened as a result. The French Revolution, with its promise of liberty, equality and fraternity, changed this, and the rights of citizenship were extended to Jews, as long as they were willing to be treated as individuals rather than as a community. The individual was king and the slogan emphasised this: *'To the Jews as individuals everything; to the Jews as a people, nothing.'*

This emancipation resulted in another transformation

of anti-Semitism. With the emergence of nationalism as the defining factor in European society in the 19th Century, anti-Semitism acquired a *racial* rather than a religious character and Jews, with their differences, were regarded as aliens in society. Dodgy scientific theories asserting that the Jews were inferior to the so-called Aryan 'races' gave anti-Semitism new respectability and popular support, especially in countries where Jews could be made scapegoats for existing social or political grievances. In this new climate, anti-Semitism became a powerful political tool, as politicians were quick to discover. In both Germany and Austria in the late ninteenth century, anti-Semitism became an organised movement with its own political parties.

The Russian Empire had restricted Jews to western regions known as the Pale of Settlement. In 1882, new laws, drafted after widespread anti-Jewish riots, or pogroms, had broken out in the Russian Pale the previous year, stripped Jews of their rural landholdings and restricted them to the towns and cities within the Pale. These measures, which crippled many Jews' activities as rural traders and artisans, spurred the emigration of more than a million Jews to the United States, Britain and other places over the next four decades.

In France the Dreyfus Affair became a focal point for anti-Semitism. In 1894 Alfred Dreyfus, a highly placed Jewish army officer, was falsely accused of treason. His final vindication twelve years later was hampered by the French military and the bitterly anti-Semitic French press. So anti-Semitism, a virus of hatred that had developed from within the church, was able to adapt to the times. One good thing is that the church has finally seen the error of its ways. Even the Catholic Church, the main villain of the piece, has finally admitted its error, officially announcing at Vatican Council II in 1965 that the Jews 'should not be presented as rejected by God or accursed'. When you look at church history, as we have done, from the early days through to Martin Luther and the Reformation, one important fact sticks out: the common person was never given a Bible to read. Bible reading and interpretation lay in the hands of the leaders and teachers, who had their own agendas to fulfil and used the Bible to justify their own vices, whether it be lust for money, power, or just good old-fashioned lust!

As soon as the Bible was put into the hands of the masses, people read it. At the very least, they found no basis for anti-Semitism, and at best they saw many justifications for a positive attitude towards their Jewish brethren. And this is still the case. Christians today are better informed than 'Christians' of yesteryear. Anyone who reads the Bible would have no excuse for reading anti-Semitism into it, unless their judgement is clouded by their own prejudice.

So, given what you have read in this chapter, do you blame the modern Jew for resisting the claims of Jesus Christ? What Jew would want to follow a religion that claims that his ancestors killed its founder and then refuses to forgive or forget? What Jew would want to follow a religion that has, over the last ten centuries, insulted you, persecuted you and slaughtered you on a whim? Given that track record, it doesn't make sense, does it? We need to understand the inbuilt distrust that Jewish people have, and to understand why, for instance, the blessed name of Jesus Christ has been such a curse for the Jews for centuries.

A salutary lesson is given in 2 Chronicles 28:9–11. An army from the Northern Kingdom of Israel had decided to act as God's army of justice against the Southern Kingdom of Judah. But they had taken it too far and had angered God in the process.

> *'But a prophet of the L<small>ORD</small> named Oded was there, and he went out to meet the army when it returned to Samaria. He said to them, "Because the L<small>ORD</small>, the God of your fathers, was angry with Judah, he gave them into your hand. But you have slaughtered them in a rage that reaches to heaven. And now you intend to make the men and women of Judah and Jerusalem your slaves. But aren't you also guilty of sins against the L<small>ORD</small> your God? Now listen to me! Send back your fellow countrymen that you have taken as prisoners, for the L<small>ORD</small>'s fierce anger rests on you."'*

If a people, whether or not they consider themselves God's people, decide to act as God's avengers without a divine mandate, all they are doing is making themselves the objects of God's wrath. May this be a warning to the church.

Finally, let's return to our Bishop of Durham. Remember, at the head of this chapter, he complained about a new prayer in the Anglican prayer book. *'This is turning the church into a scapegoat for anti-Semitism,'* he said, adding that he interpreted the prayer as God accusing the Christians of persecution and of inducing an anti-Semitic culling of the Jews.

The only possible mitigating circumstance there was, was that the Church of England wasn't directly responsible for the deeds described in this chapter. But it was the church *in* England that was responsible, God's representatives in our country. If God's current representatives feel no guilt or shame for the evil acts committed against God's kingdom of priests on British soil, there is something deeply amiss.

> **We have learnt that . . .**
> A hatred of the Jews has grown over the last nineteen centuries from within the Christian world. It is an anti-Semitism that has nothing to do with the teachings of Jesus but everything to do with a corrupted church that took it upon itself to punish the alleged 'Christ killers'.

NOTES

1 This article can be found at http://www.ekklesia.co.uk/content/news_syndication/article_040714prys.html
2 William of Tyre, *The History of Godefrey of Boloyne and of the Conquest of Iherusalem* (Hammersmith, Kelmscott Press, 1893).
3 More of how they came to these conclusions, since termed 'Replacement Theology', is detailed in my book *The Land of Many Names*.
4 Rigg, J.M., *Select pleas, starrs, and other records from the rolls of the Exchequer of the Jews, AD 1220–1284* (London, B. Quaritch, 1902).
5 'Professions of Faith Extracted from Jews on Baptism: Laws of Erwig', from Leg. Vis. 12.3.14.
6 Marcus, J., *The Jew in the Medieval World: A Source Book: 315–1791* (New York, Athenaeum, 1973).

Chapter 5

Dhimmis

They were two half-brothers with very different destinies. The Bible makes this clear. The first-born, Ishmael, would become the father of twelve rulers, who would become a great nation (Gen. 17:20). The second-born, Isaac, would inherit the everlasting covenant given to his father, Abraham (Gen. 17:19). This covenant promised him many descendants, the land on which he stood, and a legacy of blessing the nations through one of those future descendants.

The Muslim holy book, the Qur'an, says it differently. Firstly, Abraham (Ibrahim) is distanced from his Jewish roots and Christian heritage:

'Ibrahim was not a Jew nor a Christian but he was (an) upright (man), a Muslim, and he was not one of the polytheists' (Qur'an 3:67).[1]

Then when it recounts the episode of Abraham's intended sacrifice of his son, the son's identity is left ambiguous.

'And when he attained to working with him, he said: O my son! surely I have seen in a dream that I should sacrifice you; consider

84

then what you see. He said: O my father! do what you are
commanded; if Allah please, you will find me of the patient ones'
(Qur'an 37:102).

Muslims *assume* this son is Ishmael, the first-born, though
the Bible explicitly states it is Isaac.

'Then God said, "Take your son, your only son, Isaac, whom you
love, and go to the region of Moriah. Sacrifice him there as a
burnt offering on one of the mountains I will tell you about'"
(Gen. 22:2).

Muslims go on to say that Jewish or Christian scribes later
doctored the Bible, and that the son described as the
favoured one was originally Ishmael.

It's an important point because the consequence of this
testing of Abraham was that this son became known as the
child of promise and inheritor of the blessings. If it's Isaac,
then Isaac's seed is the blessed seed; if it's not, the
blessings go to Ishmael's seed. It's important because
there are implications concerning who inherits the
Promised Land and whether the faith of Ishmael's seed
(Islam) or of Isaac's seed (Judaism or Christianity,
depending on your perspective) is the true faith.

These points only became an issue when Islam, through
conquest, became the dominant faith of the Middle East in
the seventh century AD. When Muhammad first started
formulating this new religion, he was strongly influenced
by the Jews and Christians around him. He spoke of one
God, just as the Jews did, and this caused him to look
favourably on them.

And then came the experience at Medina. At that time
about half of the population of this city were Jews, who
lived in harmony with the Arabs there. One of the first
things he did was strike a covenant with the Jewish

inhabitants, promising good relations. He then set out to win them over, as is indicated by a verse in the Qur'an:

> *'And certainly We gave the Book and the wisdom and the prophecy to the children of Israel, and We gave them of the goodly things, and We made them excel the nations' (45:16).*

Muhammad tried to gain converts among the Jews, but ultimately failed to win them over. Because of this he broke away from them in AD 624 and broke his covenant with them, justifying his actions in the Qur'an:

> *'And if you fear treachery on the part of a people, then throw back to them on terms of equality; surely Allah does not love the treacherous' (8:58).*

As his influence grew in Medina, so the lot of the Jews took a familiar turn – in AD 627 his followers killed between six hundred and nine hundred Jewish men and divided the women and children among themselves.

The Qur'an sets the tone for Muslim attitude toward Jews.

> *'And abasement and humiliation were brought down upon them, and they became deserving of Allah's wrath; this was so because they disbelieved in the communications of Allah and killed the prophets unjustly; this was so because they disobeyed and exceeded the limits' (2:61).*

> *'And the Jews say: The hand of Allah is tied up! Their hands shall be shackled and they shall be cursed for what they say. Nay, both His hands are spread out, He expends as He pleases; and what has been revealed to you from your Lord will certainly make many of them increase in inordinacy and unbelief; and We have put enmity and hatred among them till the day of*

resurrection; whenever they kindle a fire for war Allah puts it out, and they strive to make mischief in the land; and Allah does not love the mischief-makers' (5:64).

Islam divides the world into two parts. First is the *Dar al-Islam* ('house of Islam'), the part of the world where Islam holds sway and Islamic law is in force. The rest of the world is the *Dar al-Harb* ('house of war'), where all is fair game except the 'People of the Book'. As 'People of the Book,' Jews were protected under Islamic law in those early days. As *dhimmis* (protected ones), Christians and Jews were allowed a place in Islamic society, as subordinates to the Muslim conquerors. Peoples subjected to Muslim rule usually had a choice between death and conversion, but Jews and Christians, who adhered to the scriptures, were allowed to practise their faith, albeit in acknowledgement of the superiority of their Muslim masters. They had to pay an annual poll tax and had to live with some stringent regulations. They were forbidden to criticise the Qur'an, Islam or Muhammad, to seek to convert a Muslim or to touch a Muslim woman. They couldn't take public office and couldn't bear arms. They were not allowed to ride horses or camels, to build synagogues or churches taller than mosques, to construct houses higher than those of Muslims or to drink wine in public. They had to show public deference toward Muslims, always yielding them the centre of the road, and were not allowed to give evidence in court against a Muslim. *Dhimmis* were also forced to wear distinctive clothing, which from the ninth century took the form of a yellow star for Jews.

In general the Jews were treated better by the Muslims than by the Christians, and did not suffer persecution on the scale inflicted by the Christians. Nevertheless, although they were able to live in relative peace and thrive culturally and economically, their position was never totally secure, and changes in the political or social climate would often lead to persecution, violence and death. There were massacres and forced conversions in North Africa and Spain in the twelfth century perpetrated by the fanatical sect of the Almohads. In 1066, a Jewish vizier was assassinated in the Berber kingdom of Granada, Spain, and afterwards the entire Jewish community of 5,000 souls was wiped out by the Muslim mob. In the thirteenth century the Islamic empire began to crumble, battered by Genghis Khan and his Mongol army, followed by the Moguls, Ottoman Turks and Almihades among others. It was all but over by the sixteenth century. Muslims still held sway in many pockets throughout the Near East and North Africa, but not as part of a great empire.

By the nineteenth century, the lot of Jews in Muslim countries had hardly improved. Jews in most of North Africa were forced to live in ghettos, and in Morocco, which contained the largest Jewish community in the Islamic world, Jews were made to walk barefoot or wear shoes of straw when outside the ghetto. Even Muslim children participated in the degradation of Jews, by throwing stones at them or harassing them in other ways. The frequency of anti-Jewish violence increased, and many Jews were executed on charges of apostasy.

The situation worsened further in the twentieth century, with the troubles in the Middle East as a result of Jews returning to the Promised Land. In 1947, the Syrian delegate to the United Nations warned: *'Unless the Palestine problem is settled, we shall have difficulty in protecting and safeguarding the Jews in the Arab world.'* Until 1948, Jews had lived in most of the Arab Muslim countries of the Middle East. In most cases they had been there more than a thousand years before Islam even existed. From 1947, hundreds of Jews in Arab lands were killed in government-condoned rioting, leaving thousands injured or dead and millions of dollars' worth of Jewish property destroyed. In 1948 Jews were forcibly ejected from Iraq, Egypt, Libya, Syria, Lebanon, Yemen, Tunisia, Morocco and Algeria, with property worth tens of billions in today's dollars confiscated. Of the 820,000 Jewish refugees created by this situation, 590,000 were absorbed by Israel.

Now that there has been a resurgence in the more militant expression of Islam, accompanied by a frenetic output from Muslim scholars, we can look deeper for further insights into Muslim opinions of Jewish people. One area worthy of consideration is eschatology, their view of the end-times. I am indebted to Tony Pearce, author of *Light for the Last Days*, for the article 'Islam & the Second Coming',[2] on which the following discussion is based.

If you're surprised that there is such a thing as Muslim eschatology, you'll be astounded to know that Muslims also believe in the second coming of Jesus. They don't get this from the Qur'an, but instead from their traditional writings, the *Hadiths*. One such *Hadith* speaks of Jesus going to Jerusalem with a lance in his hand with which he will kill the Antichrist.

> *'Then he will kill the pigs, break the cross, demolish oratories and churches and kill Christians except those who believe in him . . . There will be such security in his time that lions will lie down with camels, leopards with cattle and wolves with sheep. Youths and boys will play with snakes without harming them or being harmed by them. Then he will tarry on the earth for as long as God wills – perhaps for 40 years. Then he will die and the Muslims will pray over him and bury him.'*[3]

We see here elements that would be familiar to Christians, but there are subtle differences. The Bible account is changed and given a different meaning to fit in with

Islamic thinking. It is not only the accounts that have been changed, but also the spirit behind them. A proper understanding of the biblical prophecies should inspire us to a concern for unbelievers and a desire to see them saved from 'the wrath to come' by belief in the Gospel of peace and reconciliation with God through the Messiah Jesus. Islamic groups looking for the end of days are motivated in the opposite direction. One such group, *Hizb ut Tahrir*, has been active in British universities, calling on British Muslims to 'fight Jews and kill them' in order to hasten the end of days. They also believe that when Jesus comes again, he will kill all the Christians (except those who believe him to be merely God's servant or messenger rather than the Son of God). There is a *Hadith* which says that when Jesus returns, *'even the rocks and trees will say, "O Muslim, here is an unbeliever. Kill him!" Hence Allah will cause all unbelievers to perish.'*[4]

The Muslims claim that the difference between their account and ours is that we have 'changed the books' (i.e. our Bible is not the original message but the Qur'an is). However, in the Qur'an, which was written about six hundred years after the New Testament, Muhammad actually recommended Muslims to observe the *Taurat* (Torah) and the *Injil* (Gospel) (5:68). He did not say anything about the books being changed, a Muslim doctrine which was introduced much later when contact with Christians showed them that their version of the stories differed from the original accounts found in the Bible.

There is a hugely influential international gathering of Muslims every year. Called the *Organisation of the Islamic Conference* (OIC), it comprises fifty-six Islamic states, and its aim is to safeguard the interests and ensure the progress and well-being of their peoples and those of other Muslims the world over. The first meeting was on 25

September 1969, when it was proclaimed that the Conference was primarily concerned *'in absolute priority, with liberating Jerusalem . . . from Zionist occupation.'*

The Jews and Jerusalem have been an abiding focus of the Islamic world ever since. We must ask why. Is this just the usual anti-Semitism? Why is Jerusalem so important? It certainly wasn't for Muhammad, who never visited it, except in a dream, and who did not write about it in the Qur'an. For an answer we must delve again into Islamic end-time theology.

As I said earlier, Muslims believe that Jesus will return. The bad news is that they have a very different view of Jesus from that held by Christians. The Muslim Jesus is not the Son of God who atoned for our sins through his death, only to rise again in victory over death. Instead they believe he is just a prophet, albeit a lesser one than Muhammad. This Muslim Jesus will return, so they believe, but the scenario is not the Christian one.

It involves a period of religious turmoil, when a figure called the *Mahdi* appears, 'riding on a white horse'. He will set up his kingdom in Jerusalem (yes, you heard it right – not Mecca or Medina or Cairo) and will be opposed by the *Dajil*, a Jewish 'beast', accompanied by thousands of other Jews, who will be like a rapacious dog, hoping to occupy the city. He will eventually be slain by *Isa* (Jesus) on his return, and the 'day of salvation' will be established. This is the official position of Islam on the end-times and is all described in the influential Muslim book *The End Times and the Mahdi*, by Harun Yahya.

This is the real reason why Jerusalem is important to Muslims: it's not about the past (as there are no foundational Muslim ties to the city), it's about the future. Jerusalem, in the world's eyes, has been the stumbling block to peace in Israel, but despite what the world has been told, it's not because of any historic Muslim associations with the city, it's simply because that's where they believe Islam is finally going to be declared the true faith. One thing is clear – Jerusalem is *the* big issue in the Middle East, and there should be no confusion over this.

Modern Islamic anti-Semitism started in the 1930s, as a result of the rise of Jewish immigration to the Promised Land. Let's turn our attention to Haj Amin al-Husseini, a typical product of those times. He was a member of the al-Husseini clan, one of the two major Arab dynasties in Palestine. These were the days of European colonialism, and Britain and France managed to control most of the Middle East between them. Haj Amin al-Husseini was appointed Grand Mufti of Jerusalem by the British in 1921. He was a Muslim extremist and violently opposed Zionism, as the following activities will show us:

- In August 1929 he inspired a massacre of Jews praying at the Western Wall, their holiest place in Jerusalem.
- During the Second World War he moved to Germany and became associated with Hitler. He worked on the assumption that since they both had the same hated enemies (the Jews), they could be friends. If only he had known what Hitler thought of him (a member of a sub-race) and what his fate would have been under the Third Reich!

In the view of al-Husseini and his ilk, all Jews were fundamentally evil, dedicated to the destruction of Islam. Muslim extremists still hold this view today.

The Muslims' holy book, the Qur'an, did the Jews no favours, with plenty of verses speaking against them. If Muslims have shown negativity to the Jews, they can honestly claim that they are only following the teachings of the Qur'an. At least this is a more honest position than that taken by Christians who read hatred of the Jews in their Bible, when it plainly isn't there.

But it's not all bad news. There are small pockets of hope that show what may be possible in the future. One such story appears in the book *Israel: The Mystery of Peace*, by Julia Fisher, in the chapter 'From Algeria to Jerusalem'.

It is the story of Marcel Rebiai, born into an Algerian Muslim family but brought up in an orphanage, where he was taught to hate the Jews (as well as the Americans and the French). After running away he became a street child, until he was rescued and taken to Switzerland. He later became a drug addict, but then God rescued him and gave him a mission. God called him to Israel and helped bring about *The Community of Reconciliation*, working to bring Jews and Arabs together in love. Here he speaks of their aims:

> *'We have experienced massive opposition and violent assaults from both Islamic fundamentalists and Jewish Orthodox groups. But this has not stopped us. We also experience lives being changed and reconciliation and hope becoming a reality for our Jewish and Arab friends. This encourages us to fully invest our lives, because we believe according to Isaiah 19:24–25 that the day will come when God will make the two peoples a blessing for the whole world. We are working towards the fulfilment of this promise.'*

So there is hope. Jews and Arabs (those who can trace themselves back far enough) are half-brother nations, *Semitic*, descendants of Noah's son, Shem. There's more to unite them than to divide them. Yet perhaps no people in the modern age are so divided. Why should this be? As we shall show later, the answer can only be seen in the unseen, in spiritual realms.

> **We have learnt that . . .**
> Although there has been a history of Islamic anti-Semitism, starting with Muhammad himself, Jews historically were treated better by Muslims than by Christians, living as *dhimmis*, 'protected ones', albeit as second-class citizens.

NOTES

1 The Qur'an quotes are taken from University of Virginia on-line Qur'an at http://etext.lib.virginia.edu/toc/modeng/public/HolKora.html
2 You can see this article at http://www.lightforthelastdays.co.uk/docs/islam/2nd_coming.html
3 Al Hendy, *Kanzol 'Ummal*, vol. 17–18, *Hadiths* nos. 1014, 994, 808, 1020 et al.
4 Hafiz Ibn Hajar, *Fath-ul-Bari*, vol. VI, 450.

Chapter 6

The Chosen People

For countless centuries Christians viewed Jews as parasites, devils and pariahs. But there is some good news: they haven't all wanted to wipe out Jews. It has been said that in 1589 an English Christian, Francis Kett, was burned alive, his only crime having been to insist that the Jews would some day return to their land, an idea he got from reading the Bible. Things were soon to improve, with the emergence in the seventeenth century of the Puritans, who were so thoroughly Hebraic in their worldview that the Old Testament made something of a comeback in the Christian landscape. Concern for the Jewish people was not exactly an unconditional love, but rather was based on their end-time expectations. Their reading of scripture indicated to them that Jesus would only return to this earth once the Jewish people were restored to their Messiah and to their land. In fact two English Puritans, Joanna and Ebenezer Cartwright, petitioned the British and Dutch governments in the mid-1600s to be allowed to become *'the first and the readiest to transport Izraell's sons and daughters in their ships to the Land promised by their forefathers, Abraham, Isaac, and Jacob for an everlasting Inheritance'*. Oliver Cromwell was even urged to accept the Jews back into England, a country seemingly devoid of Jews at that time, as it was thought that the Jews needed to be dispersed to all nations in order for God's end-time plans to unfold. To the Puritans, the Jews (as well as themselves) were God's chosen people, and so there began the first reversal of Jewish fortune in the Christian world since the Pope stopped being Jewish.

There seem to be three possible motivations for this swing in attitude towards the Jewish people. The first is a common humanity, idealised at the time of the Enlightenment, when the idea went around that all men were created equal and should be treated as such. These people would accept Jews for the people they were as individuals, rather than seeing them as tainted by the negative images circulating in the medieval 'Christian' world. Although this is actually a biblical and a Christian (as well as Jewish) ideal, you don't need to be religious to follow it. These people would say, *'Jews are my friends'* and actually mean it, rather than saying, *'My best friends are Jewish'* and not mean it for one minute!

The second motivation is a humanitarian response to the various injustices handed out to the Jews, a sort of a 'protective' impulse to compensate for the normal 'destructive' impulses characteristic of society as a whole. Again this is a biblical principle, and again you don't need to be religious to hold it. These people would say, *'You may hate them but I am proud to have them as friends.'* People in this category, such as Winston Churchill, have had an undisguised admiration for the achievements of the Jewish people.

The third motivation is strictly a biblical, Christian one. It identifies Jews as the chosen people of God, still chosen after all these years, despite what the church may say. These people see Jews as central to God's plan for humanity and their destiny as a key issue. These people are responsible for the movement known as *Christian Zionism*. These people would say, *'We must be friendly to the Jews; they are special people.'*

Zionism is a word used to describe the yearning in the Jewish heart to return to the land of Israel. It became a Jewish political movement in the mid- to late 1800s. Yet British Christians had beaten them to it. As Christian Zionists, they had been advocating the restoration of a Jewish state in the land for the previous two hundred years. As already noted, it started with the Puritans, but it didn't end there: a spark, it seems, had been ignited in the British Christian soul.

In 1733 the brilliant scientist Sir Isaac Newton suggested in his *Observations upon the Prophecies of Daniel and the Apocalypse of St John* that the end-time scenario necessitated that another nation assist the Jews to return to their Promised Land. Later that century another British scientist, Joseph Priestly, wrote, *'The land is uncultivated and ready to receive you, but the Turks control it. Their power must first fall. Therefore, I earnestly pray for its dissolution. But it may not happen for sometime.'* Books by other Christians followed, expressing the same sentiment.

Christian Zionism sprang from the explosion of interest in biblical prophecy, particularly that focused on the Second Coming of Jesus. The Jews were at the centre of it all. Without their role in the matter there could be no Second Coming. The Christian Zionists' theology demanded a return of the Jews to their Promised Land and it expected their complete spiritual restoration. An early pioneer of this thinking was Charles Simeon, who regarded the conversion of the Jews *'as perhaps the warmest interest of his life'*.

Here are some quotes from influential Christians of that time and earlier:

Charles Haddon Spurgeon:

'I think we do not attach sufficient importance to the restoration of the Jews. We do not think enough of it. But certainly, if there is anything promised in the Bible, it is this.'[1]

John Calvin:

'When the Gentiles shall come in, the Jews also shall return from their defection to the obedience of faith; and thus shall be completed the salvation, ... which must be gathered from both; and yet in such a way that the Jews shall obtain the first place, being as it were the first born in God's family, as Jews are the first born . . .'[2]

Jonathan Edwards:

'When they shall be called, that ancient people, who alone were so long God's people for so long a time, shall be his people again, never to be rejected more. They shall be gathered together into one fold, together with the Gentiles . . .'[3]

Matthew Henry:

'Now two things he exhorts the Gentiles to, with reference to the rejected Jews: to have a respect for the Jews, notwithstanding, and to desire their conversion. This is intimated in the prospect he gives them of the advantage that would accrue to the church by their conversion.'[4]

A distinguished gallery of writers, clerics, journalists, artists and statesmen accompanied the awakening of the idea of Jewish restoration in Palestine. Lord Lindsay, Lord Shaftesbury, Lord Palmerston, Benjamin Disraeli, Lord Manchester, George Eliot, Holman Hunt, Sir Charles Warren, Hall Caine, Robert Murray McCheyne – all appear among the many who spoke, wrote, organised support or put forward practical projects by which Britain might help the return of the Jewish people to Palestine.

There were some who even urged the British government to buy Palestine from the Turks and give it to the Jews to rebuild.

When in 1798 Napoleon invaded Egypt and the territory including modern-day Israel, the British were concerned, both politically and spiritually. Politically, because they feared that trade routes to India would be blocked, and spiritually, because evangelical Christians were starting to ponder the subject of the restoration of Israel.

At that time a German Jew, Joseph Frey, became a believer in Jesus the Messiah. He trained as a missionary, intending to work in Africa, until he visited Whitechapel, London, and saw the state of the poor Jews who lived there. There and then he decided to work there with Jewish people, beginning at a small Methodist chapel in Aldgate.

But soon he realised he needed more resources, both human and financial, to do the job properly, and he managed to find like-minded people. In May 1809 they formed the *London Society for the Promotion of Christianity Amongst The Jews*, which was a bit of a mouthful and so was also known as the *London Jews Society*. It was soon endorsed by the great and good of the land. Supporters included William Wilberforce and Charles Simeon, and the Duke of Kent was to become its patron.

Other missionary organisations directed towards the Jews were formed in London at that time, such as the *Mildmay Mission to the Jews*. At the beginning of each year Hudson Taylor, the legendary missionary to China, sent them a cheque, inscribed on the back of which were the words of Romans 1:16, '*I am not ashamed of the gospel of Christ: for it is the power of God unto salvation to everyone that believeth; to the Jew first . . .*' John Wilkinson, of the mission organisation, would then write a cheque for the same sum and promptly return it marked '. . . *and also to the Greek'*. The *Barbican Mission to the Jews* operated as a medical mission, particularly to the poorest Eastern European Jews. In the window of the mission hall were displayed tracts in Yiddish, which would be dispensed along with the medicine as a condition of the free treatment.

In 1868, Benjamin Disraeli became British Prime Minister. It was a turning point for Jews in England and, curiously, it could never have happened were it not for a petulant act of his father, Isaac D'Israeli. After a row with his synagogue, Bevis Marks, he refused to have his son bar mitzvahed. Instead, he had Benjamin baptised. Thus it was that a Jew, now a paid up member of the British establishment and the Church of England, was able to reach the highest office in the land. Around the same time the great British novelist George Eliot wrote *Daniel Deronda*, concerning the struggle of a Jew to retain his identity. The book, which dealt with the idea of Israel as an eventual homeland for the Jewish people, was read by a Russian Jew named Yehuda Perlman, who agreed with this central concept. This man was to become Eliezer Ben Yehuda, the person responsible for the rebirth of the ancient Hebrew language in the modern nation of Israel.

In Yad Vashem, the Holocaust memorial in Jerusalem, there is an area known as the *Avenue of the Righteous among the Nations*, a parade of trees planted in honour of those Gentiles who stood by the Jews in their sufferings during the Holocaust. By January 2003, 19,700 Gentiles had been so honoured.

One such was Francis Foley, head of the passport division in the British Embassy in Berlin in the 1930s. He helped thousands of Jews to leave Nazi Germany by handing out visas willy-nilly, without the necessary red tape.

Similarly honoured was the whole nation of Denmark. Virtually alone among the defeated nations, the Danish government reached an agreement with the Nazis that no Jews would be harmed and none were, all being transferred safely to Sweden and out of harm's way. For the Israelis, the action of Denmark *'stands out in the history of the period as an outstanding act of moral and political responsibility'*.

Now here is our own 'Avenue' of Righteous Gentiles, a list of Gentile Christians who have bucked the trend in Christendom and have displayed a sincere 'philo-Semitism', a genuine love for the Jewish people, a love that showed itself as direct action, sometimes with negative consequences for themselves.

Corrie ten Boom
Corrie ten Boom lived during the Second World War as the daughter of a watchmaker in Holland. She had a brother and two sisters and lived in a home where the Bible formed the centrepiece of their lives, used as a living guidebook rather than as a doorstop or a weapon of hate. Her family were poor but happy, and by all accounts nothing very remarkable happened to this lady until she was just about to approach her middle-aged years. Then the Nazis came to town. Anti-Semitism first reared its ugly head in the form of a young German apprentice who worked in their shop. For no apparent reason other than having joined the Nazi party (which I suppose was a pretty good reason), he had started to regularly beat up the old man who'd worked at the shop for years. For a kindly and godly lady it was a profound shock to see how unjustified hatred can flare up. The apprentice was immediately sacked. The following year the Nazis invaded Holland and her life was to turn upside down.

The ten Boom family had many Jewish friends, including the local rabbi, and were appalled at what they saw going on around them. Jews now had to wear a six-pointed star on their clothing at all times and were slowly being forced out of society – banned from restaurants, jobs, even their own homes. The family were also to witness Jews being taken away in trucks, officially to 'work camps' but in reality to death camps.

But this was no ordinary family. Rather than turn a blind eye, they actively prayed for opportunities to show solidarity with the Jews. Their chance came and they gave shelter to three homeless Jews, despite the extreme dangers attached to this act. Corrie ten Boom, then in her fifties, became a resistance leader of the Dutch underground, with special responsibilities for finding safe havens for the Jewish population of her town. The watchmaker's shop became a centre of resistance activity, with all members of the ten Boom family actively participating, motivated by their Christian faith and the knowledge that they were doing God's work.

After nearly two years Corrie had built up a network of eighty workers and had helped hundreds of Jews. But things were getting harder and harder as the Nazis increased their grip, and the dangers were immense. One day they were visited by a captain in the Nazi army of occupation; it was the same German apprentice they had sacked years earlier. Although his suspicions were fuelled by old resentments, he found nothing suspicious in this innocent watchmaker's shop. But this luck had to give out, and they were finally betrayed by a local man, Jan Vogel. The Gestapo arrived and rounded up the family. They were then split up and Corrie and her sister Betsie were placed in prison, in solitary confinement for their 'crimes'. Her father, a frail old man, was also imprisoned and died ten days later. After three months the sisters were both transferred to Vught Concentration Camp. It wasn't a death camp, rather one where you worked until you dropped. Corrie was employed making radios for the

Germans. Soon this camp was dismantled and the 'guests' were moved to a far more sinister and dreaded place, Ravensbruck Concentration Camp in Germany. The work there was much harder, the regime far crueller. While she was an inmate her spirit was never broken; her faith sustained her, even after her sister died in captivity. She lived totally for others in the camp, even the guards, sharing her faith. She survived the camp by virtue of a clerical error – if she had stayed a week longer she would have been put to death along with all the other women of her age.

Corrie ten Boom lived the rest of her life as a missionary to the world, travelling extensively and speaking to audiences in every part of the globe, telling them about her faith and her experiences in Ravensbruck. It was because of her kindness to Jewish people, without any regard for her personal safety, that she lived through those years of hell in prison and concentration camps. Yet not once did she regret her actions and she died with a prayer to God on her lips.

Lord Balfour

This man has been described as perhaps the most effective British friend the Jews have ever had. I'm sure you've all heard of the *Balfour Declaration*, the piece of paper that gave official British recognition of the need for a Jewish homeland in Palestine. Well, here is the man behind it. His full name was Arthur James Balfour and he was British Prime Minister in 1902. He wasn't very good at the job and lost office in 1905, but bounced back when he became Foreign Secretary during the First World War.

Politically, he had made many friends with influential Jews, including Theodore Herzl, the first 'Zionist'. His most significant friendship, though, was with Chaim Weizmann, the Jewish chemist and Lenin look-alike.

When they met in 1914 Balfour stated that the Jewish question would remain insoluble until either the Jews in Britain became entirely assimilated or there was a normal Jewish community in Palestine. In the meantime the British offered Uganda as a possible homeland for the Jews. This was rejected.

Balfour asked Weizmann why Uganda was rejected, and why the Jews were so hung up on Palestine. Weizmann responded by asking why the British were hung up on London. Balfour replied that the British currently had London but the Jews did not have Jerusalem. Weizmann replied, *'We had Jerusalem when London was a swamp.'* That was enough to persuade Balfour to begin to argue for Palestine for the Jews.

As the First World War progressed, Weizmann made himself invaluable to the British war effort through his discovery of a process to produce synthetic acetone, a chemical needed to make cordite, a naval explosive. His reward was the Balfour Declaration, contained in a letter to Lord Rothschild, the most prominent Jew of the day. Here is the letter:

2 November 1917

Dear Lord Rothschild,

I have much pleasure in conveying to you, on behalf of His Majesty's Government, the following declaration of sympathy with Jewish Zionist aspirations which has been submitted to, and approved by, the Cabinet.

'His Majesty's Government view with favour the establishment in Palestine of a national home for the Jewish people, and will use their best endeavours to facilitate the achievement of this object, it being clearly understood that nothing shall be done which may prejudice the civil and religious rights of existing non-Jewish communities in Palestine, or the rights and political status enjoyed by Jews in any other country.'

I should be grateful if you would bring this declaration to the
knowledge of the Zionist Federation.
Yours sincerely,
Arthur James Balfour

Lord Balfour had a Christian upbringing and it was his deep familiarity with the Old Testament, rather than a particular love for the Jewish people, that motivated his favourable attitude towards them. It mustn't be forgotten that as Prime Minister in 1905 he had introduced the Aliens Bill, to limit Jewish immigration to Britain, at a time when they were still being severely persecuted in the east. A decade later he seems to have softened his attitude, saying, *'The treatment of the race has been a disgrace of Christendom'*, and viewed the establishment of a Jewish state as a way of making amends. Although he didn't live to witness the eventual birth of the State of Israel, his name is commemorated throughout the land in streets, a forest and a *moshav* (agricultural cooperative).

Lord Shaftesbury
The idea of a Jewish homeland in Palestine, though present in Jewish hearts since the start of the dispersion, really started to take hold of Christian minds at the start of the nineteenth century. It all started (probably) with the Frenchman, Napoleon Bonaparte, who promised Palestine to the Jews. The trouble is that he failed to conquer the land, so it wasn't his to give away! But nice touch, Napoleon, your heart was in the right place. After this, however, particularly in Britain, we start to see many prominent people – writers, artists, statesmen – all of one mind on the Jewish issue: the need for a Jewish homeland. Lord Shaftesbury was the most loved politician and one of the most effective social reformers in nineteenth century England. He became interested in the Jews through his

study of biblical prophecy – he was so keen to understand the Old Testament that he forced himself to learn Hebrew for that very purpose. He became convinced that the Jews should be encouraged to return to Palestine, their God-given home, and he encouraged Palmerston, the British Foreign Secretary, to do something about it politically. Such was the might of the British Empire in those days that it seems the British were free to do what they liked, because as a result of Shaftesbury's prompting, Michael Alexander, a Jewish Christian, was sent to the Holy Land as the first Bishop of Jerusalem. Although this man only lived for another couple of years, and the scheme only lasted for fifty years, it represented a solid achievement in the quest for an eventual Jewish homeland in Palestine.

Lord Shaftesbury never gave up his vision and constantly prompted key movers of nineteenth-century Britain to share this vision. It was said that he was sent a ring from Jerusalem engraved with the Hebrew words of a Psalm: *'Oh, pray for the peace of Jerusalem; they shall prosper that love thee.'* He wore this ring for the rest of his life. Curiously the statue of Eros in Piccadilly Circus, London, was dedicated to him, which doesn't make that much sense as he did little to promote the cause of minor Greek deities!

Winston Churchill
This man needs no introduction. Younger readers will remember him as the inventor of the 'two-fingered gesture', the *V-for-Victory* sign. Older readers and students of history will acknowledge him for encouraging the bulldog spirit of the British people and rousing them, through his inspiring speeches, to victory (with help from the Americans of course) in the Second World War.

Winston Churchill was a great friend of the Jewish people, whom he admired greatly. In fact he was known as 'the last romantic Zionist Gentile'. As early as 1908 he spoke of *'full sympathy . . . with their aspirations of establishing a Jewish homeland'.*[5] Sometimes, among the British Government, he seemed to be their only friend. Here are some relevant episodes from his life:

- In 1921, when asked by the Canadian Prime Minister what he thought the implication of the Balfour Declaration was for the British people, Churchill replied that it was *'to do our best to make an honest effort to give the Jews a chance to make a national home for themselves'.*

- In 1922, motivated by his pro-Zionist views, Churchill ended the ban on immigration of Jews to Palestine (although in the following year the British reduced the proposed homeland by 75 per cent, to form Trans-Jordan for the Arab Palestinians).

- Churchill said that the Jews were the most remarkable race on the earth and their religious contribution was *'worth more than all other knowledge and all other doctrines'.*

- As Prime Minister during the Second World War he was in favour of increased Jewish immigration to Palestine, to save them from Nazi atrocities, but was over-ruled particularly through the efforts of the Foreign Secretary, Anthony Eden, who was too worried about what the Arabs would think of it, even though many were pro-Nazi.

- Churchill was the only real supporter in both Allied governments of the bombing of the Auschwitz death camp factory.

- Churchill was the only supporter of the idea of a Jewish strike force against the Germans. He got his way and the 25,000-strong Jewish Brigade was formed. The experience gained by these Jewish fighters became invaluable when they subsequently had to fight for their existence during the Arab-Israeli wars.

David Lloyd George

Yes, it's another British political figure, this time the Prime Minister at the time of the First World War. Here was another man convinced by his reading of the Bible about the destiny of the Jewish people and their rights to the Holy Land. His inclusion in this list is due to the willing role he played in the political dramas taking place at the time, particularly concerning the efforts of Chaim Weizmann and other Jewish Zionists. It is clear that it was well within his power to block the Balfour Declaration, yet to his credit he chose to sponsor it.

David Lloyd George was one of the prominent politicians targeted by Chaim Weizmann, who also 'nobbled' Winston Churchill and Lord Balfour, creating Zionists of the three of them (and therefore deserving the highest honour paid to him when he was made the first president of the State of Israel).

It was when Lloyd George had taken over the War Office from Lord Kitchener (he of *Your country needs you* war poster fame) that things really got moving. More resources were diverted to the war effort in the Middle East, culminating in the taking of Palestine from the Turks. Things got even better when Lloyd George took over as Prime Minister from the anti-Semitic Asquith. It just wasn't realised at the time that the man now elected to run the country was a philo-Semite and a fervent Zionist. In fact after a war meeting with prominent financiers, including Lord Rothschild, he was heard to remark, *'Only the old Jew made sense.'* Weizmann and Herbert Samuel, another Jewish politician, cleverly worked on Lloyd George by reminding him of how Palestine was the same size as his own homeland, Wales, and constantly mentioning place names in the Holy Land that they knew would be familiar to him, as they knew he was a Bible-thumper. But I'm sure Lloyd George, not a stupid man, was a willing convert to the cause.

When the First World War was over, both Lloyd George and Lord Balfour were determined that if any good were to come out of this pointless war it would be to establish a home for the Jews. Lloyd George even told Weizmann at one time that *'Palestine was the one interesting part of the war.'*

Orde Wingate
Here was a truly great friend of the Jews, and a practical one too – he taught them how to fight! Captain Charles Orde Wingate of the British Army was an ardent Christian Zionist and during the 1936–1939 Arab riots in Palestine he undertook the training of special Jewish commando units, which worked under cover of darkness by the name of the *night squads*. Many of Israel's future military leaders had their initial military experience under this man. Moshe Dayan had this to say about him: *'There were times when he would march on, driven by an iron will. He had an unshakeable belief in the Bible. Before going into action, he would read the passage in the Bible relating to the places where we would be operating and find testimony to our victory – the victory of God and the Jews.'*

He was well loved by the Jews in the land, who named him *Ha-Yedid*, 'the friend'. Unfortunately the British high command wasn't too pleased with the activities of this maverick and he was withdrawn from Palestine in 1939 with the following endorsement in his passport: *'The bearer . . . should not be allowed to enter Palestine.'*

His dream was always to lead the army of the future Jewish state, but sadly he was to die in a plane crash in Burma in 1944. He loved the Jews right up to the end; a year before his death he wrote in a letter to a friend: *'If I forget thee, O Jerusalem...'* This brave man is now commemorated in Israel by a children's village, a College of Physical Education, a forest, and a square in Jerusalem.

Lewis Way

Here was another product of the religious awakening of the nineteenth century. Although he was well off and a member of a respected and prominent family, the main part of Lewis Way's life was spent on one single purpose, the restoration of Israel.

In 1817 he made an extensive journey through Europe at his own expense, visiting Holland, Germany, Russia and Poland. On the basis of the reports he made to his missionary society, the *London Society for Promoting Christianity amongst the Jews*, missions were opened in Poland, Holland and Germany. When in Russia, he met the Emperor, Alexander I, with the express intention of reminding Russia of her 'Christian' duty to help restore the Jewish people to their homeland. Ironically, the subsequent treatment of Jews by the Russian people, through state-sponsored pogroms, did drive out many, though not just to the Promised Land but also to Britain, America and other places.

In 1821 he placed his country home at the disposal of his missionary society, as a training school for Jewish Christians. He died in 1840 and was eulogised by a later historian thus: *'The best earthly friend whom Almighty God has vouchsafed to the Society. God raised him up for this great work and furnished him with all the talents which it required; learning, genius, wealth, fervent piety and a heart overflowing with love for His ancient people.'*

William Hechler

The father of modern Zionism was an Austrian Jew called

Theodore Herzl, who in his pamphlet *The Jewish State*
began to turn the far-fetched idea of a Jewish land in
Palestine into a believable reality for many Jews. What
isn't so well known is that he probably couldn't have done
it without a British Christian Zionist, William Hechler.
Here was a remarkable man, who had even prophesied
that the Jews would return to their land by the start of the
twentieth century.

One day Hechler found a copy of Herzl's *The Jewish
State* and became so excited that he searched him out and
they became firm friends. Herzl considered Hechler to be
a religious zealot but became interested when he
discovered Hechler could provide him with an
introduction to the German Kaiser and the British Prime
Minister. This latter relationship was to bear fruit, as we
read earlier. Hechler was to work alongside Herzl until
the death of the Austrian.

It is interesting and significant that apart from Corrie ten
Boom, all of the above were British. It is not a contrived
list, born out of misplaced patriotism. It is a lot easier to
compile a list of anti-Semites, believe me, a list that would
span the centuries and the continents. But you have a
more limited choice when you wish to list the 'philo-
Semites', and two factors do stand out sufficiently to make
them statistically probable – adherence to the Christian
faith and a British birth. Interestingly, it seems that the
period of greatest 'philo-Semitism' shown by the British
people coincided with the rise and flourishing of the
British Empire. But this attitude seemed to change after
the Second World War: something to do with Arab oil, I
believe. Is it a coincidence that the subsequent lamentable
record of the British Government towards Israel has
paralleled the dramatic and swift collapse of the British
Empire? It's worth a brief consideration, surely?

> **We have learnt that . . .**
> Some Christians, particularly in England, began to reverse the trend and view the Jews more favourably. This movement, starting with the Puritans and reaching its peak in the nineteenth century, was instrumental in the creation of Christian Zionism, which believes in the restoration of the Jews, God's 'chosen people', and their return to their Promised Land.

NOTES

1 Spurgeon, Charles Haddon, *The Restoration and Conversion of the Jews*, vol. 1, 214.
2 *Calvin's Commentaries*, vol. 19, Epistle to the Romans (Baker House), 434–40.
3 *The Works of Jonathan Edwards*, vol. 1 (Banner of Truth Trust, 1976), 607.
4 Rom. 11:12, 15. *Matthew Henry's Commentary*, vol. 6 (MacDonald Publishing Company), 448–53.
5 *Jewish Chronicle*, 3 September 2004, 25.

Chapter 7

Conspirators of Zion

There is a website that acts as the mouthpiece of the *International Jewish Conspiracy* (IJC) (http://www. internationaljewishconspiracy.com). It speaks of the mysteries of kabbalah, Jewish infiltration of both fundamentalist Christianity and the Moonies, secret signs and a newsletter from the Elders of Zion.

Sinister, indeed. In fact, it's a hoot, and intentionally so, as it's a spoof. A clue is a news story on the home page, speaking of an ancient document recently found, *The Book of Shlomo*, which tells of the time Moses parted the Atlantic Ocean and visited Bermuda for a one-week vacation with room, half-board and discounted windsurfing lessons included in the price of the parting! But I wonder how many were taken in by this clever, tongue-in-cheek website, before the penny dropped. That's the problem; that's the tragedy.

We love conspiracies, whether they involve moon landings, the deaths of presidents, movie stars or princesses, or fevered speculations about trivia dreamed up by media moguls to increase circulation figures. Then there are the outlandish theories about who exactly is pulling the strings in the world today. Many candidates have been put forward, from the disguised lizards of David Icke to the secret societies of the Freemasons, the Illuminati, the Jesuits, the Bilderburg Group, the Knights Templar, the Rosicrucians, the Club of Rome and . . . yes, of course, the Jews.

And we're not talking of just one alleged Jewish conspiracy; there's a whole swathe of them. Whispers are heard of the *Protocols of the Elders of Zion*. Zionism is seen as a front for world domination, with the Israeli secret service (*Mossad*) pulling the strings. Then there are the United Nations, the New World Order, the communists, the International Monetary Fund (IMF), the World Bank and the world's press. Apparently all have been sucked into the Jewish web! Jews have been put forward as the primary cause of most of the major problems that have weakened European society in the past two hundred years, such as the First and Second World Wars, communism, socialism, liberalism, capitalism, mass immigration, forced integration, racial preference laws and media bias. Such busy bees we've been!

The *Protocols of the Elders of Zion* is probably the best-known weapon in the armoury of anti-Jewish conspiracy nuts. It is also a complete forgery, but why should the truth get in the way of a good yarn? It is claimed to be the minutes of a meeting of Jewish leaders at the first Zionist congress in Basel, Switzerland, in 1897 (or, as some say, a graveyard in Prague), when the Jews were hatching an audacious plot to take over the world.

What it actually was is not that easy to follow. It seems to be based on a pamphlet written at the turn of the twentieth century by a forger in Russia as a way to discredit reforms in that country and bolster the influence of the Tsar. This forger took material from a satire on Napoleon III by Maurice Joly and from a novel by

Hermann Goedesche, a nineteenth-century German anti-Semite. The final form of the Protocols first appeared in Russia in around 1905, becoming a best-seller by 1920 and promoted in the USA by none other than Henry Ford, who when he wasn't building cars was ranting and raving about Jews. It was first exposed as a forgery by Philip Graves of *The Times* in 1921, but not before one Adolf Hitler had had a chance to read it and believe it.

Possibly after noticing that car sales were plummeting in parts of New York, Henry Ford was forced to make a public retraction, admitting that the book he had written in 1920, *The International Jew*, was based on the Protocols.[1] He said:

> '*I am deeply mortified that this journal, which is intended to be constructive and not destructive, has been made the medium for resurrecting exploded fictions, for giving currency to the so-called Protocols of the Wise Men of Zion, which have been demonstrated, as I learn, to be gross forgeries, and for contending that the Jews have been engaged in a conspiracy to control the capital and the industries of the world, besides laying at their door many offences against decency, public order and good morals... I deem it to be my duty as an honourable man to make amends for the wrong done to the Jews as fellow men and brothers, by asking their forgiveness for the harm which I have unintentionally committed, by retracting, as far as lies within my power, the offensive charges laid at their door by these publications, and by giving them the unqualified assurance that henceforth they may look to me for friendship and good will . . .*'

Mind you, this didn't stop him being the first American recipient of a Nazi award bestowed upon non-Germans in 1938!

Of course, anti-Semites of all persuasions are not going to let the fact that it is pure fiction get in their way, as it is freely distributed these days by Muslim hate groups and neo-Nazis. One recently broadcast Egyptian TV series, *A Knight Without a Horse*, is even based partly on it – there's a scene in which three old Jews are sitting in a room filled with religious artefacts, heavily perspiring and conspiring as they plot and plan. This series sparked a debate at the highest level between the presidents of Israel and Egypt, the latter stating, *'The series is no more than an artistic comment on the history of Egypt and the region at large produced and directed in accordance with Egyptian laws.'*

Naturally, the Nazis made good use of the Protocols as a justification for their paranoid hatred of the Jews. Since then, their main use has been as justification for Arab nationalism and Muslim hatred against the State of Israel. The Protocols were translated into Arabic from the French edition probably in the late 1920s, and by the 1950s the forgery could be found all over the Arab world, from Cairo to Beirut. They were even authenticated by Egypt's President Nasser, whose brother published a new edition in 1968 under the title *Brutukulat Hukama Sahyun wa-Ta'alim at-Talmud* ('Protocols of the Learned Men of Zion and Teachings of the Talmud').

Commenting on the Jewish (or Zionist – same thing really) conspiracy to take over the world, one article, translated from Russian to English and featured on an anti-Jewish Islamic website,[2] ranted and raved about the evil Jews and then summarised the situation thus:

'The only reliable method of putting matters in order for literally everyone, both Jews and the entire Gentile population of the Earth, is that the Jews should renounce their aims of taking over the world – in fact, that means that they should renounce Zionism – and that they should be resettled in Israel.'

It just shows how anti-Semites have hijacked the word 'Zionism', corrupted its intended meaning of a Jewish yearning to return to their homeland, and turned it into a sinister conspiracy to take over the world. The real point of Zionism *is* to resettle in Israel; renouncing it will defeat the whole point of it!

Most of the other so-called Jewish conspiracies are simply variations on the theme of strategies to achieve world domination over the last few hundred years. Let's summarise a few of them:

- In 1775, Jews financed the American Revolution.
- In 1933, Jews conspired against the Germans and caused the Second World War.
- In 1990, Jews conspired against the Iraqis and caused the Gulf War.
- In 1999, Jews conspired to incite the bombing of Serbs in Serbia. (The Serbian Defence League website is subtitled *Documenting Zionist genocides on Serbs*.)
- In 2001, Jews were the real instigators of 9–11.
- Jews have instigated, supported and financed the First World War, the Cold War, the Korean War and the Vietnam War as part of a perpetual Jewish war against the rest of the world.
- Jews control the United States government through an organisation known as ZOG (Zionist Occupation Government).

Just think: if all the above is claimed to be true, it speaks as much about Gentile stupidity as it does of Jewish cunning, if the non-Jews have blindly allowed themselves to be led through every major calamity in history by just 0.21 per cent of the population. It was this kind of thinking that made the 'Final Solution' against the Jews acceptable to Germans in the 1930s. It was forced into their minds through every possible channel of propaganda until the individual was left unable and unwilling to disbelieve it.

It made it possible for ordinary Germans to turn a blind eye, first to the expulsions and exclusions, then to the shop-burnings and Jew-baiting, and finally to people being dispatched on journeys in cattle wagons to far-off places in Poland, never to be seen again.

Finally, the most repulsive, sinister and intellectually corrupt claim of all: that the Holocaust never happened, despite thousands of Jewish (and Gentile) eyewitnesses, Nazi documents, newsreels and other photographic evidence. It is suggested that the Holocaust was a Jewish conspiracy, a lie intended simply to engender sympathy from the world for the plight of the Jews and their yearning for a homeland of their own. One such Holocaust-denier, David Irving, sued an American academic, Deborah Lipstadt, in 2002 for claiming that he is a 'Hitler partisan' who twists history to cast the German dictator in a better light. He lost his case and his house and was declared bankrupt.

The Jews have indeed been a busy people, conspiring to take over the world through their cunning and deviousness, while the rest of the world stands in wide-eyed innocence, powerless to resist them!

The concept of the *scapegoat* is a Jewish one. It was one of the two goats received by the Jewish high priest in ancient Jerusalem on the Day of Atonement, as described in Leviticus 16. The priest laid his hands on the scapegoat as he confessed the people's sins, before sending it out into the wilderness. Today, a person who has been blamed for something which is the fault of another is referred to as a scapegoat. The Jews have always been a convenient scapegoat for others, allowing their enemies to ignore their own shortcomings or giving them a way to vent their frustrations and misfortunes. Blaming Jews for every low point in human history, from the Black Death to communism to the Second World War, may make one feel superior and justified, but it's doing nothing more than feeding a lie.

> *'So justice is driven back, and righteousness stands at a distance; truth has stumbled in the streets, honesty cannot enter. Truth is nowhere to be found, and whoever shuns evil becomes a prey. The Lord looked and was displeased that there was no justice'* (Is. 59:14–15).

Talking of conspiracies, what is less well known are the ones that are *against* Jewish people. The machinations and subterfuges initiated against the nation of Israel by friend and foe alike could furnish plots for a dozen Frederick Forsyth novels. In fact the insistence on the existence of a Jewish conspiracy to control the world is a conspiracy itself, if the truth be told. One day the truth *will* be told and then there will be many heads hung in shame. Until that day we'll just have to put up with the fact that ZOG controls the White House, the Pope is a secret Jew and the Hollywood film industry is just a front for the Israeli Secret Service.

We have learnt that . . .
Anti-Semitism has been able to adapt with the times, particularly when feeding imaginations on various Jewish conspiracies to control the world.

NOTES

1 More information about Henry Ford and his relationship with the Jews can be found at http://www.jewishvirtuallibrary. org/jsource/anti-semitism/ford.html
2 For examples of such Islamic anti-Semitism go cautiously to www.radioislam.net

Chapter 8

The Jews

As the advert says, *It does what it says on the tin*. So it is with this chapter. Here we concern ourselves with the Jewish people, focusing on what they have contributed to the world as a people group among all other people groups. But first we embark on a whistle-stop tour of their times in exile.

As we read earlier, the Jews were truly spread worldwide, driven from country to country by waves of persecution. For every country that banished them from its borders, another reluctantly absorbed them. But how did they live and how did they flourish in these strange lands? What was it that kept them together as a distinct people, knowing that assimilation – absorption into the general population – would have been a better bet for individual, if not racial, survival?

The one thing that they had that bound them together was the *Torah*, the teachings. The *Torah* is the first five books of Moses – Genesis, Exodus, Leviticus, Numbers and Deuteronomy – known to the Jewish people as the *Chumash*, or the *Pentateuch*. Sometimes the term is extended to include the whole Hebrew Bible, called the

Tanakh, the Old Testament. It can also include the oral as well as the written law, bringing other Jewish writings such as the *Mishnah*, the *Midrash* and the *Talmud* into the equation.[1] This final definition is the one most used by Orthodox Jews, Jews who take their religion the most seriously. They would define the *Torah* as both the initial reason for *Galut*, the exile, and the reason for its continuation. The *Torah* was entrusted to the Jews as a sacred responsibility and their failure to meet its demands resulted in *Galut*. That is the accepted position within Judaism. The continuation of exile is also attributed to their self-confessed failure to spread *Torah* principles to the nations surrounding them, to be a *blessing to the nations*. That's how they consider the working-out of the Abrahamic Covenant, as defined in Genesis 12:2–3.

So the *Torah* was both a blessing and a curse to them. It provided them with a strict moral framework for living as strangers and pariahs in foreign communities. It ensured a high degree of literacy and cleanliness, setting them apart from the ignorant, superstitious masses who viewed them with such disdain.

A cornerstone of the Jewish community in *Galut* was and is the family home. In the absence of a temple, the rabbis referred to the home as a substitute, a place of sanctuary set aside for holy purposes, such as prayer, study and serving the community. The Sabbath and Festivals in particular drew these elements together, with the dinner table as central focus. As well as eating and drinking, the other sacraments of Bible study, songs of praise and prayer took place around this table. It cemented the family together, with the father as head, his wife at his side, making sure the next generation received adequate instruction in the way of *Torah*. Every father took on this responsibility as a sacred duty thoroughly validated by biblical teaching.

'These commandments that I give you today are to be upon your hearts. Impress them on your children . . .' (Deut. 6:6–7).

Although Jewish people through the ages have kept their identity and distinctiveness as a community bound by the *Torah*, the last fifty years or so have seen many changes. As the world opens up and communities mix more freely, Jews are diffusing into the culture of their host nations, taking on their morality and ethical framework. Although there are still strongholds of Jewish orthodoxy, holding on to the (perceived) restrictions of *Torah*, each new generation of Jews is sucked further into the secular society, with as much danger of losing their distinctiveness as other immigrant communities. In medieval times almost 100 per cent of Jews in Europe would have been observant of the *Torah* – what we today would call *orthodox* – but that figure has now dropped to around 10 per cent. The rest either celebrate their religion in a more 'culturally-sensitive' sense, as liberal Jews, or would just not celebrate their Judaism at all, save for the occasional Passover, Yom Kippur and a weekly subscription for their burial plot.

If you are still wondering what possible role Jews could have in God's plans during the *Galut*, the exile, when the church considered them cursed and hated by God, consider this: without them and their faithfulness and their stubbornness, you would not have the Bible today. I am not referring to the original writers of the Bible, but to the driven, obsessed people who again and again painstakingly made copies of aged manuscripts, ensuring that by the time Bibles were printed in English, the Old Testament portion was guaranteed virtually 100 per cent free of error. Meet the *Masoretes*, Jewish scribes from the first century to the ninth century. There's no room here to give their whole story, but just one aspect of their working practice will serve to illustrate their contribution to biblical scholarship. Consider the fact that when they copied from an old scroll to a fresh parchment, no word or letter could be copied from memory and, if a single tiny mistake was made, the parchment would be destroyed and they would start again. Thank goodness our standards have dropped, otherwise this particular book would never have reached you! This behaviour of the *Masoretes* may seem over-obsessive to us, but it ensured that the manuscripts used as sources for the Bibles we read today were extremely accurate, a fact that has since been borne out by the discovery of the Dead Sea Scrolls.

When is a Jew a Jew?

Until recently, Jews have been a people without a land, a people in exile. They lived then, as do most Jews today (unless they are living in Israel), in the *Galut*. Although the biblical tradition states that 'Jewishness' comes through the male line (which is why the genealogies, apart from the odd exception, only showed the men), the rabbis stated that to be a true Jew you need, as a minimum requirement, a *Yiddishe Momma* (a 'Jewish mother', for those unfamiliar with the subtle nuances of Yiddish). This deviation was brought about through practical reasoning. During times of extreme persecution, the identity of one's father was sometimes doubtful and, even when the father was known, one didn't particularly want one's child brought up as a Russian Orthodox or as a Cossack. You always knew who your mother was, and even if you had the blond hair and blue eyes of an unknown father, you would still be brought up under the protection of the Jewish community as one of its own. Of course, intermarriage has also occurred on a voluntary basis and explains why Jews from a given country, whether it be Germany, France or Ethiopia, in many cases look just like

Gentiles from the same country. When the Ethiopian airlift arrived in Israel at the time of the African famines, many a voice was heard to exclaim, *'But they're schwartzers!'*, only to be answered, *'Yet heimische schwartzers, nu?'* Roughly translated into the Queen's English this becomes, *'I say, these chappies are coloured chappies!'* followed by, *'Oh yes, my good man, but they're one of us!'*

Others have become Jews through marriage (e.g. Elizabeth Taylor) or preference (e.g. Sammy Davis Junior). To become a Jew, a non-Jew has to undertake some formal study. In the orthodox tradition a man still has to undergo circumcision and a woman has to learn how to make a good chicken soup (I think, though I may be wrong). It's a lot easier in the reform tradition, which just goes for the basic studying and a formal declaration. If this is all in the context of a marriage, it is sometimes referred to as a 'mitzvah marriage', defining it as a *mitzvah* or a 'good work', in that it is adding to the household of Israel.

It's not so straightforward to stop being a Jew. Of course you can simply deny your background and not tell anyone. This is quite easy to do if you move solely in Gentile circles, though your racial characteristics, to say nothing of ritual scars, may prove a bit of a give-away! Sometimes, particularly when you're going through a time of personal rebellion, you say to yourself, *'I'm an individual, I don't want to be labelled.'* You don't want the cultural baggage of a 'different tradition', particularly one that, as a rule, is looked down upon by your peers. I know of at least three cases in my family alone in which first names or surnames have been changed to hide the person's Jewish identity. Many entertainers, particularly those from immigrant families, have changed their names in order to further their career. It is doubtful that Sid James (of *Carry On* fame) would have been so endearing to the British public if he had kept his original name – Solly Cohen!

The Board of Deputies of British Jews, the governing body of Jews in this country, has highlighted *assimilation*, in which for one reason or another Jewishness is lost, as the biggest threat to the Jewish community today. It has been estimated that in America, about half of Jewish marriages now involve a non-Jewish partner, with less than one-fifth of the Gentile partners converting to Judaism. This is an unprecedented situation and could be seen, at worst, as a form of national suicide on the part of the Jews of the *Galut*. At this rate, surely Jews outside Israel could end up as a marginalised minority community with little or no influence on society.

During the nineteenth century there were many cases of Jews becoming Christians, in name only, in order to further their career in society at large, usually in the realm of politics. Examples of this were Benjamin Disraeli, the British Prime Minister, and Karl Marx, the philosopher, who were both brought up as 'Christians' by Jewish parents. In earlier times, during the Spanish Inquisition, some Jews in Spain and Portugal accepted a form of conversion to Christianity as an alternative to death, though still preserving Jewish traditions in private. These were the *Marranos*, mentioned earlier. In the *Talmud*, one of the books of Jewish tradition, it says that *'an Israelite, even though he sin, remains an Israelite'*. This basically means that once born a Jew, you remain one, whatever mischief you've been up to and whether you like it or not.

Many books have been written exploring the issue of Jewishness and trying to define whether a Jew belongs to a nation, a race, a tradition, a religion or a state of mind. I don't wish to add any more to this discussion except to mention one interesting fact . . .

When is a Jew not a Jew?

The best test you can have of your 'Jewishness' is to see if the State of Israel would grant you citizenship. In 1948 the Knesset, the parliament of Israel, formulated the 'Law of Return'. This states that any Jew can receive Israeli citizenship the moment he or she sets foot on Israeli soil. It doesn't matter whether you believe or not in God or the Bible, or whether you're a communist, an astrologer or even a convert to Hinduism: as long as you've got the papers to prove you're a Jew, you're welcome.

There is only one group of people who are definitely *not* welcomed with open arms, and they are Jewish Christians, or Messianic Jews. In 1989, the Israeli Supreme Court decided that Messianic Jews were not eligible to immigrate to Israel under the Law of Return. It was (and still is) considered by the Jewish community as a whole that Jewish converts to Christianity are no longer Jews. They are now considered Christians, as if a foreskin had grown back, and knowledge of Yiddish, chicken soup recipes and *Shabbat* prayers had been mystically blotted out, replaced by a new zeal for car maintenance, Irish stew and hiking.

Seriously, one should not joke about such things. Instead we must try to understand why it should be, why the highest court in the land of Israel should be moved to completely and utterly disown any Jew who has professed a faith in Jesus, but to accept any Jews who have embraced Buddhism, Hinduism, atheism, Satanism, even Islam! Interestingly, at the time of the new law a poll was published in the *Jerusalem Post*, which found that 78 per cent of the Israeli public favoured Messianic Jews coming into Israel under the Law of Return, provided that the immigrants were really of Jewish lineage, held to their historic heritage and served in the army when called upon to do so.

It was OK if you have no belief in God, or believe that God is another name for Nature, or even believe that God has three heads and a tail! All of these were acceptable; Israel would have welcomed you with open arms. But if you believed that the Jewish Messiah had come and his name was Jesus Christ (actually *Yeshua Ha Mashiach*, his proper Jewish name), in the eyes of the Jewish establishment you had 'lost your Jewishness'. You had become the enemy, or, in the eyes of the orthodox, you'd died and, if you came from an orthodox family, a funeral would have been conducted for you!

These were strong reactions indeed. You could have been a mass murderer or a compulsive adulterer, but you could still be Jewish and would have been allowed your very own place in the State of Israel – albeit in a maximum-security prison. But in the eyes of a state that claims, as a whole, not to be religious, your Jewishness could have been stripped away like the skin of a banana simply because you believed in something they disagreed with. Now take one step back and with a clear, rational mind consider for a moment what you've just read. Why should one's beliefs provoke such a reaction? Is it rational, or is there something going on here that needs further investigation?

The reason for the decision by the Israeli Supreme Court was simply a fear, a justifiable fear born out of the lamentable treatment Jews had received for centuries at the hands of the 'Christian' church, culminating (but not ending) in the Nazi Holocaust, an event considered by many Jews as a Christian-inspired event. The church has so much to answer for. Thanks to many in the Christian world who have woken up to the sins of the past, the Christian Zionists and others with a sincere love for the Jewish people, there has been some reassurance for the Israeli government that Christendom has changed with the times. These days, the worst kinds of anti-Semitism (those involving physical violence) seem to be coming more from the Muslim world. This is not to say that 'Christian' anti-Semitism is no more; it's just that it doesn't have the power to threaten Jewish lives, although it is, sadly, still very active behind the scenes, poisoning minds and souls.

There's something special about these folk

Even the most rabid anti-Semite would have to admit that there is definitely something special about these folk. We read the statistics in the Introduction:

There are just over 13 million Jews worldwide (2000 figures), indicating that about 0.21 per cent of the world is Jewish – about one person out of every 470. So the expectation is that 0.21 per cent of the world's scientists, musicians, entertainers and writers would, on average, be Jewish. Yet in the period since the mid-nineteenth century about 25 per cent of the world's scientists have been Jews, and in 1978, over half the Nobel Prize winners were Jewish. Over 50 per cent of the main contributors to human progress that year coming from 0.21 per cent of the population!

Now, a roll of honour. Here is a selection of people of Jewish ancestry who have 'made it' in the world at large in the last couple of hundred years.[2]

Writers

Isaac Asimov, Saul Bellow, Judy Blume, Anita Brookner, Jackie Collins, Edwina Currie, Noam Chomsky, John Diamond, Andrea Dworkin, Harlan Ellison, Ben Elton, Nora Ephron, Martin Gilbert, Albert Goldman, William Goldman, Zoe Heller, Joseph Heller, Arthur Koestler, Judith Krantz, Erica Jong, Franz Kafka, Primo Levi, Ira Levin, Norman Mailer, David Mamet, Arthur Miller,

Dorothy Parker, Boris Pasternak, Harold Pinter, Chaim Potok, Marcel Proust, Harold Robbins, Jack Rosenthal, Philip Roth, Oliver Sacks, J.D. Salinger, Hugh Schonfield, Will Self, Sidney Sheldon, Neil Simon, Isaac Bashevis Singer, Muriel Spark, Danielle Steele, Tom Stoppard, Jackie Susann, Leon Uris, Irving Wallace, Elie Wiesel.

Actors, entertainers and personalities
Edward G. Robinson, John Garfield, Lee J. Cobb, Kirk Douglas, Tony Curtis, Robin Williams, Melvyn Douglas, Bette Midler, Richard Dreyfuss, Walter Matthau, Lawrence Harvey, Winona Ryder, Gene Wilder, Maureen Lipman, Dustin Hoffman, Richard Benjamin, Elliot Gould, Michael Douglas, Anouk Aimee, Sarah Bernhardt, Al Jolson, Eddie Cantor, Barbra Streisand, Alma Cogan, Helen Shapiro, Milton Berle, George Burns, Danny Kaye, Lenny Bruce, the Marx Brothers, Bud Flanagan, Sid Caesar, Woody Allen, Harrison Ford, Mel Brooks, Sophie Tucker, Dinah Shore, Eddie Fisher, Neil Sedaka, Paul Simon, Art Garfunkel, Topol, Billy Crystal, Marty Feldman, Jerry Lewis, Sid James, Jack Benny, Frankie Vaughan, Bob Dylan, Elkie Brookes, Neil Diamond, Leonard Cohen, Harry Houdini, Howard Werth, Peter Green, Paul Kossoff, Paula Abdul, Jackie Mason, Theda Bara, Fanny Brice, Bernard Bresslaw, Bernie Winters, Alexei Sayle, Joan Rivers, Lionel Blair, Marjorie Proops, Claire Rayner, Uri Geller, Ruby Wax, Dani Behr, Tania Bryer, Muriel Gray, Ron Moody, Warren Mitchell, David Baddiel, Jeff Goldblum, David Schwimmer, Leonard Nimoy, William Shatner, Saatchi & Saatchi, David Copperfield, David Suchet, John Suchet, Lou Reed, Mark Knopfler, Goldie Hawn, Vanessa Feltz, Stephen Fry, Debra Winger, Vidal Sassoon, Linda McCartney, Marc Bolan, David Schneider, John Bluthal, Miriam Karlin, Miriam Margolyes, Janet Suzman, David Kossoff, Alicia

Silverstone, Caprice, Rachel Stevens, Gwyneth Paltrow, Amy Winehouse, Nigella Lawson, Ben Stiller, Jack Black, Roseanne Barr, Lenny Kravitz, Jerry Springer, Judd Hirsch, Jason Biggs, David Blaine, Sacha Baron Cohen, Ronnie Ancona, Henry Winkler, Jerry Seinfeld, Zero Mostel, Adam Sandler, Paul Newman, Jo Brand, Krusty the Clown, Sharon Osbourne, Madaleine Kahn, Rodney Dangerfield.

Producers/directors
The Warner Brothers, William Fox, Louis B. Mayer, Samuel Goldwyn, Louis Selznick, Adolph Zukor, Jack and Harry Cohn, Jesse Lasky, Lew Grade, Lord Delfont, Steven Spielberg, Sam Wanamaker, Michael Winner, David O. Selznick, Joseph Mankiewicz, Alexander Korda, Billy Wilder, Roman Polanski, Richard Benjamin, Peter Bogdanovich, James L. Brooks, Ethan and Joel Coen, David Cronenberg, Cecil B. DeMille, Sergei Eisenstein, Stephen Frears, William Friedkin, Sam Fuller, Lawrence Kasdan, Stanley Kubrick, John Landis, Fritz Lang, Mike Leigh, Richard Lester, Barry Levinson, Sidney Lumet, Jonathan Lynn, Sam Mendes, Frank Oz, Sydney Pollack, Otto Preminger, Harold Ramis, Carl Reiner, Rob Reiner, Ivan Reitman, John Schlesinger, Don Siegel, Oliver Stone.

Politics
Benjamin Disraeli, Sir Herbert Samuel, Anatoly Scharansky, Leslie Hore-Belisha, Manny Shinwell, Leon Blum, Leon Brittain, Lord Young, Nigel Lawson, Gerald Kaufmann, Malcolm Rifkind, Michael Howard, Greville Janner, Golda Meir, Henry Kissinger.

Business/commerce
Milton Friedman, the Rothschilds, the Montefiores, the Samuels, the Sassoons, the Goldsmiths, the Montagus, the

Mocattas, George Soros, Michael Dell, Alan Sugar, Robert Maxwell, Roman Abramovich, Mitchell Glazer.

Music and art
Itzhak Perlman, Isaac Stern, Yehudi Menuhin, Sir George Henschel, Gustav Mahler, Felix Mendelssohn, Jacques Offenbach, Georges Bizet, Benny Goodman, George and Ira Gershwin, Irving Berlin, Richard Rodgers, Oscar Hammerstein, Leonard Bernstein, Lionel Bart, Jerome Kern, Larry Adler, Sammy Cahn, Jacob Epstein, Marc Chagall, Jerome Kern, Alan Jay Lerner, Frederick Loewe, Stephen Sondheim, Burt Bacharach, Marvin Hamlisch, Lucian Freud, Roy Lichtenstein, Vladimir Ashkenazy, Don Black, Aaron Copland, Jerry Goldsmith, Michael Kamen, Carole King.

Science, medicine and philosophy
Albert Einstein, William Herschel, Niels Bohr, Albert Michelson, Heinrich Hertz, James Franck, Paul Ehrlich, Robert Oppenheimer, Edward Teller, Isidor Rabi, Claude Levi-Strauss, Ludwig Wittgenstein, Martin Buber, Karl Marx, Heinrich Heine, Baruch Spinoza, Sigmund Freud, Alfred Adler, Jonas Salk, Carl Sagan, Chaim Weissman, Jacob Bronowski, Benoit Mandelbrot, Nostradamus, Max Born, Richard Feynman, Wolfgang Pauli.

Sport
Harold Abrahams, Mark Spitz, Gary Jacobs, Ronnie Rosenthal, Eyal Berkowitz, Joel Stransky, Phil Cohn (as we're struggling in this category, I'm putting forward my grandfather, a useful boxer in the 1920s in the East End, I'm told, and the first and last time he'll ever be written about).

OK, it's just a list of names, but to put it into perspective let's just look at one area, the musical theatre. The following musicals were composed by Jews: *Fiddler on the Roof, Oliver, West Side Story, The Sound of Music, Show Boat, Porgy and Bess, South Pacific, The King and I, Annie Get your Gun, Cabaret, Camelot, Carousel, Chicago, A Chorus Line, Fame, 42nd Street, Funny Girl, Gigi, Godspell, Guys and Dolls, La Cage aux Folles, Les Misérables, A Little Night Music, Little Shop of Horrors, Mary Poppins, Miss Saigon, My Fair Lady, Oklahoma!, The Producers* and *The Wizard of Oz*. It's harder to find one that *isn't* Jewish! The only major composer in the most prolific period (mid-twentieth century) who wasn't Jewish was Cole Porter, who explained how he made the leap to Broadway theatres: *'I'll just write Jewish tunes.'* Irving Berlin, one of the major songwriters of the twentieth century, was to write *White Christmas* (ironic, eh?), *Easter Parade* (even more ironic), *God Bless America* and *There's No Business Like Show Business*. In 1924 it was remarked that *'Irving Berlin has no place in American music. He is American Music.'*

And if you think this is a bit contrived and selective, here's a well known answer to anti-Semites by the Jewish comedian, Sam Levinson.

'It's a free world; you don't have to like Jews, but if you don't, I suggest that you boycott certain Jewish products, like the Wasserman test for syphilis; digitalis, discovered by a Dr Nuslin; insulin, discovered by Dr Minofsky; chloral hydrate for convulsions, discovered by Dr Lifreich; the Schick test for diphtheria; vitamins, discovered by Dr Funk; steptomycin, discovered by Dr Z. Woronan; the polio pill by Dr A. Sabin and the polio vaccine by Dr Jonas Salk. Go on, boycott! Humanitarian consistency requires that my people offer all these gifts to all people of the world. Fanatic consistency requires that all bigots accept syphilis, diabetes, convulsions, malnutrition, infantile paralysis and tuberculosis as a matter of principle. You want to be mad? Be mad! But I'm telling you, you ain't going to feel so good!'

How can this be?

Let's face it, most books you have read on the subject would just have left you with the above lists in order to say, *'Look at us, aren't we great! Don't the facts speak for themselves?'* But we need to say what is usually not said explicitly. There is something special about these folk! But what is it? Is it in the genes, a biologically inherited characteristic? Is it the environment, perhaps something about being herded into ghettos and forced into inward contemplation? These are definitely contributory factors, just as they are (and it has to be said) in the case of so many Afro-Caribbeans who excel in music and sport. (How many white sprinters/heavy-weight boxers/ basketball players do you know?) But Jewish people have impacted the world in so many different spheres and have influenced the thinking of the world so dramatically, that we need to look deeper. As mentioned in the Introduction, the three men who have arguably most influenced the twentieth century – Albert Einstein, Sigmund Freud and Karl Marx – were all Jewish, as were the founders of two of the main world religions, Judaism and Christianity.

The Jews. What's it all about? They seem to be at the forefront of everything, whether it's science, the media, fashion, the arts, the literary world or politics. Just look at *The Times* obituary columns and see how many Jews figure among the great and the good in our society. No wonder some paranoid malcontents look around and think 'conspiracy'! It is a conspiracy, but it's not a human one. There's no doubt about it – and this is as politically incorrect as it gets – God has sprinkled Jewish people with some form of magic dust. It's a form of grace, undeserved favour. It doesn't guarantee salvation or a spiritual high standing. It doesn't even come on condition that this gift be used for the common good. There have been Jewish gamblers, swindlers, gangsters and rogues who have used this gift for personal gain and have died in their sins. It's a mystery and, I believe, a by-product of the covenant God made with Abraham. It is hinted at in the wording of the covenant:

> *'I will make you into a great nation and I will bless you; I will make your name great, and you will be a blessing. I will bless those who bless you, and whoever curses you I will curse; and* **all peoples on earth will be blessed through you***' (Gen. 12:2–3, my emphasis).*

I believe that Jesus is the fulfilment of the above, but there are many biblical precedents for partial fulfilments of prophecy and this could very well be one of them.

Now I hope this doesn't sound arrogant, because it is not meant to be. Some things need to be spelt out; sometimes we must go beyond the expectations of polite society and restrictive political correctness and say it as it is. Black people are superb athletes and musical innovators! Asians are hard working and clever! British people are creative and stubbornly independent! Americans are energetic and marketing geniuses! The Japanese are highly productive and polite! And Jews are all of the above, except the first and the last – when was the last time you met a polite Jewish athlete (or even an impolite one)?

Just look at Israel. Look at what the people of this country, one of the youngest and smallest countries in the world, have achieved. It has a larger economy than all of its immediate neighbours combined and the highest ratio of university degrees to population in the world. Israel also produces more scientific papers per capita than any other nation and has the largest number of start-up companies in the world.

Yet in December 2001, Daniel Bernard, the former French ambassador to the UK, referred to Israel as *'that* s***** *little country'*. It seems that not everyone has felt so positive about Jewish contributions to society. We are going to meet these people in the next chapter.

We have learnt that ...
The Jews attribute their survival as a distinct people for so long to the *Torah*. It is hard enough being a Jew, but the hardest in terms of acceptance is to be a Jewish believer in Jesus. Jewish people have impacted society to an extent that goes beyond reason. We suggest that there is an element of divine favour in operation, though it is, in reality, a mystery.

NOTES

1 The *Mishnah* is a collection of Jewish tradition and teaching that was originally communicated by word of mouth from biblical times. When it was completed, commentaries known as the *Gemara* were added and both together comprise the *Talmud*. The *Midrash* is a separate collection of moral teachings, parables and legends.
2 For a fuller list (about one hundred times larger than mine) go to www.jewhoo.com

Chapter 9

Yids, Kikes and Hebes

And now for the big one. Why does the world hate Jews so much? It's a big question and we should consider what reasons people give. Is it religious, as between Muslims and Hindus in Asia? Is it about land, as with the British and Argentinian spat over the Falkland Islands? Is it economic, blaming Jews for the financial misfortunes of others? Is it because of their insularity, the way they 'stick together', just like every immigrant group in this country? How about the already-mentioned worldwide Zionist 'conspiracy' to take over the world, just like those attributed to the Freemasons, the Catholics or countless cult groups?

Think on. Historically, it has in fact been *all of these*; all have been given as reasons for hating the Jews. Yet it is my belief that it has also been none of them. That's confused you, so let me explain. Let's say you've been invited out to a party but you have absolutely no desire to go; it's a school reunion, and you were the one they all used to pick on. You need an excuse, and fast. You phone them and say you've already planned to go elsewhere. There's a silence on the phone and you panic. Your conversation continues like this: *'Oh yes, and our car's acting up . . . and my husband's feeling a bit peaky . . . and I can feel a headache coming on.'* You pile on the excuses as if the sheer quantity of them somehow makes it more acceptable for you to be absent from the party. Meanwhile your school friend has seen through all of this and is saying to herself, *'She doesn't really want to come to my party, does she?'* If you'd just given one reason and left it there, it would have been all right, but by giving excuse after excuse you create confusion and doubt in the other's mind.

Returning to my story and fitting it all together, we reach the conclusion that the many justifications given for hating the Jews are a smokescreen hiding the real situation: the truth is that people in general just don't like them. Deep down they don't really know why and are quite happy to believe any explanation put forward by others, and the more reasons the better – it helps to justify those irrational thoughts.

Yids! Kikes! Hebes! We are truly a people of many names, not all of them nice. So how does this anti-Semitism surface? Are all non-Jews natural anti-Semites? Do all anti-Semites want to kick us all into the sea? Anti-Semitism can surface in many ways and here are a few examples:

- As I take notes from the *Encyclopedia of the Jewish Religion* in the reference library, I notice that of the 420 pages, only the two pages containing the entry 'Jew' are slashed with a razor blade!
- *'Some of my best friends are Jews'* (all-time classic), usually followed by something like *'But we have rules / it's more than my job's worth / now if it were up to me, but . . .'*, then ending with the denouement concerning a golf club or a party or somewhere where the last person they'd like to see would be a Jew!

- The use of 'Jew' in expressions such as *'Don't be such a Jew'*, meaning *'Don't drive such a hard bargain'*, or as a verb, as in *'to Jew'*, meaning *'to cheat'*. I suppose we have to stifle a giggle when we discover that a 'Jewish piano' is another name for a cash register and then consider that without real 'Jewish pianos' the world would be robbed of much of its music, including 'The Star Spangled Banner', 'White Christmas', 'Easter Parade' and 'Rhapsody in Blue'.
- It can be unconscious, inasmuch as it can be handed down in a 'traditional' sense, for example in popular songs. Did you know that the origin of the affirmation *Hip Hip Hooray* is an ancient Roman chant used while Jews were being wiped out in medieval villages? The word *Hip* was originally *Hep*, an acronym for *Hierosolyma est perdita* (Jerusalem is destroyed).
- Little ditties like *'Roses are red, violets are blueish; if it wasn't for Jesus we'd all be Jewish.'* Gentiles may say, *'How odd of God to choose the Jews'*, but I would answer, *'if he hadn't so presumed, you Gentiles would be doomed!'*
- I've just discovered that 50 Jewish graves in a local cemetery have been desecrated for no special reason. Why don't you ever hear of this happening to Christian or Muslim graves?

But surely not in this day and age? You may say that, but you are making the false assumption that our society has reached some enlightened state. If you believe it is true, then it's simply that all the old hatreds and fears have dropped below the surface. The *Jewish News* of 13 August 2004 reported that there had been a rise in anti-Semitism in Britain, with more than thirty separate incidences in July alone. It was the second highest total since record-keeping had begun twenty years earlier.

Here are a few examples of such behaviour in Europe in recent times:

- In Belgium, thugs beat up the chief rabbi, kicking him in the face and calling him 'a dirty Jew'. Two synagogues in Brussels were firebombed; a third, in Charleroi, was sprayed with automatic weapon fire.
- Oxford lecturer Tom Paulin, a noted poet, told an Egyptian interviewer that American Jews who move to the West Bank and Gaza should be shot dead.
- A Jewish *yeshiva* student reading the Psalms was stabbed twenty-seven times on a London bus.
- In Italy, the daily paper *La Stampa* published a front-page cartoon: a tank emblazoned with a Jewish star points its gun at the baby Jesus, who pleads, '*Surely they don't want to kill me again?*'
- In Germany, a rabbinical student was beaten up in downtown Berlin and a grenade was thrown into a Jewish cemetery. Thousands of neo-Nazis held a rally, marching near a synagogue on the Jewish Sabbath. Graffiti appeared on a synagogue in the western town of Herford: '*Six million were not enough.*'
- In Ukraine, skinheads attacked Jewish worshippers and smashed the windows of Kiev's main synagogue. Ukrainian police denied that the attack was anti-Jewish.
- In Greece, Jewish graves were desecrated in Loannina and vandals hurled paint at the Holocaust memorial in Salonica.
- In Holland, an anti-Israel demonstration featured swastikas, photos of Hitler and chants of '*Sieg Heil*' and '*Jews into the sea*'.
- In Slovakia, the Jewish cemetery of Kosice was invaded and 135 tombstones destroyed.
- In Lyon, France, a car was rammed into a synagogue

and set on fire. In Montpellier, the Jewish religious centre was firebombed, as were synagogues in Strasbourg and Marseilles and a Jewish school in Créteil. A Jewish sports club in Toulouse was attacked with Molotov cocktails, and the words *'Dirty Jew'* were painted on the statue of Alfred Dreyfus in Paris.

Despite the impact of the Holocaust, anti-Semitism has never left Europe. It became unfashionable for a while, but now it is back, particularly – if the statistics are to be believed – in France. *'Stop saying that there is anti-Semitism in France,'* President Jacques Chirac scolded a Jewish editor. *'There is no anti-Semitism in France.'* Perhaps the following statistics will help us to understand better what is happening in France. There are approximately six million Muslims and only about 600,000 Jews presently living in France. To answer Chirac, perhaps we should say, *'Something smells very Vichy in the air'*!

Perhaps it's time for light relief, so let's have a look at some popular misconceptions, particularly from medieval times, just to show how ignorance was rife in that lamentable period of Christian history.

- Many medieval Christians actually believed that Jews had horns and a tail. This was due to a mistranslation by Jerome of a passage in the Book of Exodus describing Moses as he came down from Mount Sinai. The Hebrew used the word for a 'ray of light' shining from his forehead. This was mistranslated as 'horns'. Michelangelo actually sculpted Moses the Lawgiver with a nice set of horns.
- It was believed that Jews had a characteristic smell that would disappear as soon as they converted.
- One piece of research on the Jewish nose concluded

that it was the hereditary outcome of a habitual expression of indignation.

- Still on noses, yet another study found that most Jews do not have a Jewish nose, but a Greek nose.
- The German leader Bismarck once said that Germany's male nobility should marry Jewish women, to *'improve their race'*. (Of course, he didn't realise that such offspring would legally be Jewish, which would have created quite an interesting situation.)

'Whaddyamean?' sounds the cry. *'Some of my best friends are Jewish!'* This can be a comment delivered with full sincerity, but the body language and voice tone tell you otherwise. In fact many Gentiles, when confronted by an accusation that prompts this opening remark, are unaware of any negative feelings towards Jews. This is particularly so for Christian Gentiles. Yet it can be there, lurking in deep, dark corners of your psyche, or what the psychologist called the racial memory or archetypes. It's like that unreachable fat deposit in your sink's U-bend. It blocks the flow of water and can only be shifted by a spurt of caustic soda.

Now you're probably thinking that I'm being over-sensitive on this. Those of you from other minority cultures are used to the occasional poisonous barb or hurtful insult from the indigenous folk (even though they were immigrants once). If so, you've probably been at the receiving end of far more racism than your average Jew living in the UK in 2004.

But there is a difference in this case.

Firstly, we have to be aware of the origin of much of the negativity thrown at Jews. For example, a Christian minister was speaking to me once of financial matters and casually asked how it was that I was no good with money (a true statement, as it happens). The implication was that all Jews are experts with money; it's in their blood. And how did it get in their blood? It got in their blood because from 1066 onwards the 'Christian' rulers of our country declared that the only profession Jews were permitted to have was moneylending. So for a modern Christian to refer to this fact, albeit out of ignorance, is to refer to a past of shame and prejudice.

Even supporters of Israel are not exempt from this insidious seed within the 'British soul'. I overheard a conversation recently in which a lady was enthusing about the blessings she had received through her discovery of the Jewish roots of her faith. Her companion was telling her of dealings he was having with a Jewish company which had slapped an unexpected surcharge on some service they were offering. *'How Jewish,'* she exclaimed, and they both chuckled. This rankled with me, but I said nothing. These people were not anti-Semites by any stretch of the imagination, but they were making themselves a channel for ancient prejudices. It is curious to me that I have rarely witnessed such attitudes from young people or members of other ethnic groups. It seems to be a characteristic mainly of white English-born men of a certain age, though it is not, I stress, a feature of every member of that particular grouping. Or perhaps it's just sensitive old me!

It is worth making a brief mention of the Melanie Phillips article published in *The Spectator* on 16 February 2002, entitled 'Christians who hate the Jews'. She was reporting on a meeting of Jews and prominent Christians brought together to discuss the churches' increasing hostility towards Israel. She wrote,

> *'The real reason for the growing antipathy [to Israel], according to the Christians at that meeting, was the ancient hatred of Jews rooted deep in Christian theology and now on widespread*

display once again. . . . The Jews at the meeting were incredulous
and aghast. Surely the Christians were exaggerating. Surely the
churches' dislike of Israel was rooted instead in the settlements,
the occupied territories and Prime Minister Ariel Sharon. But
the Christians were adamant. The hostility to Israel within the
*church is rooted in **a dislike of the Jews**' (my emphasis).*

The Christians at that meeting affirming this view were
the editor of the main Church of England newspaper, the
Archbishop of Wales (now the Archbishop of Canterbury),
the Middle East representative of the Archbishop of
Canterbury and the head of a Christian institute and relief
organisation, who remarked, *'What disturbs me at the*
moment is the very deeply rooted anti-Semitism latent in
Britain and the West. I simply hadn't realised how deep within
the English psyche is this fear of the power and influence of the
Jews.'

Then there's another issue that became one of *the* news
stories of 2004, bringing Christian matters to the forefront
of everyday life. No it's not dodgy vicars or paedophile
priests, it was the launch of Mel Gibson's film *The Passion*
of The Christ. Having attended the press launch, I wrote an
article for a couple of websites looking at the effect the
film could have on the Jewish community. Here is an
extract:

'The problem is one of context. The Jewish characters (apart from
Jesus and his disciples) are continually angry at Jesus, but we
are not told of their reasons in a way we can understand. A
thorough reading of the Gospels would provide that context, but
the film, concentrating on the final 12 hours of Jesus' ministry,
only gives us brief flashbacks to the remaining 3 years of his
public life. A reading of the Gospels would also show us other
things. It would show us that the chief priests and the elders
were responsible for the whole sorry episode, for their own

reasons *(Matthew 26:3–4, Matthew 27:20)*, and it was their manipulation of the Jewish crowd that gives the impression that all the Jews present were after his blood. We are not shown that in the film; instead we were shown the Jewish people mocking him, pushing him, pelting him with stones and demanding his death, right up to Golgotha. Satan, a curiously androgynous character, makes an appearance at strategic points throughout the film, but it always seemed to be among the Jewish characters, rather than the Roman ones. It brings to mind the words in John 8:44, about "belonging to your father, the devil". Although this quote was clearly intended for the Jewish leadership, the inclusion of this scene acts to reinforce the negative view of Jews in general. When Jesus says to Pilate, "the one who handed me over to you is guilty of a greater sin", He was clearly referring to Judas, but instead we cut to the faces of the Jewish leaders, implying who the film-makers really hold responsible for the deeds of that day. In fact the only Jewish characters (apart from John and the Marys) who show any sympathy were some women, mostly dressed suspiciously in black, with a curious resemblance to Catholic nuns!

'I would in no way recommend this film to Jewish unbelievers, for the reasons already stated. It could have been so different. If Gibson had only included Jesus' assertion in John 10:17–18, "The reason my Father loves me is that I lay down my life – only to take it up again. No one takes it from me, but I lay it down of my own accord," either at a prominent part of the action, or as text at the end of the film, then this would have spoken volumes about his desire for good relations between the Christian and Jewish communities. By not doing so, for all the good this film will do, it will only add to the curse of anti-Semitism that is again growing across the globe. What Christians must realize is that, in the eyes of the Jewish community, this film just serves to reinforce their views on the Christian attitude to Jewish people. They see Christians raving about this film and they see the "same old same old". Despite all of their proclamations over *recent years, they still hate us! A Christian watching the film is inclined to feel sympathy for Jesus and contempt for the Jews. For many Jews watching the film, it is the other way round. How many Jews will this entice into the Kingdom? Very few, I suspect.'*

The main point I was trying to make was not really about the film itself, but the insensitivity shown by the Christian community to the Jewish community. The overriding impression was that nothing must be allowed to get in the way of the Gospel opportunities given by the film and there was even an implication, in some quarters, that all negativity shown towards the film was of the devil! Well, no revival came as a result of the film and the Jewish community has a long memory.

You, dear reader, must decide if any of this touches a familiar chord with you. There are warnings in scripture that are also worth considering. Some are considered in the final chapter of this book, but I'll mention a couple of important ones here.

First, there's the old faithful, often-quoted verse.

*'I will bless those who bless you, and **whoever curses you I will curse**; and all peoples on earth will be blessed through you'* *(Gen.12:3, my emphasis).*

Much has been written on this, focusing for example on what happened to Germany after the war (split into two), to Britain when it started favouring the Arabs in the Middle East conflict (lost its empire), and to Poland when it kicked out the Jews in medieval times (didn't realise that they were actually running the country!). It's a controversial and debatable subject, but that doesn't mean we should discount it.

> 'For this is what the LORD Almighty says: "After he has honoured me and has sent me against the nations that have plundered you – for **whoever touches you touches the apple of his eye** – I will surely raise my hand against them . . ."' (Zech. 2:8–9, my emphasis).

The Jews, on account of their ongoing relationship with God, have a certain standing before Him. There is a sense that crimes against Jews are in fact crimes against God. Here are a couple of biblical examples to show what happened to two particular tyrants who did touch 'the apple of His eye'.

The first is Pharaoh, King of Egypt at the time of the Exodus. The Jews (or Israelites as they were then known) were there as forced labour. Pharaoh feared their numbers and doubted the loyalty of his immigrant workforce in times of war. The harder he worked them, the greater their numbers became (where did they get their energy from?) and he decided to limit their size by killing all newborn boys. But, the Bible tells us, he missed one: Moses.

Despite witnessing countless miracles at the hands of God, working through Moses, Pharaoh refused the Israelites a termination of employment. In fact he made them work even harder. This action didn't exactly endear the people to Moses, whom they blamed for all this misfortune. But God had other plans and decided to show His power by visiting a series of plagues on Pharaoh and the Egyptian people. Water was changed to blood, frogs hopped down from the sky and gnats were formed from dust. Pharaoh's magicians had no trouble duplicating the first two, but the third one had them stumped and they advised their boss to stop his stubbornness and let the Israelites go. But would he listen? No! Then came clouds of flies, followed by a terrible plague on the livestock. But still Pharaoh would not listen. Next came horrible boils. It seems that the magicians had these on their feet, as we read that they couldn't even stand up in front of Moses. Then came the worst hailstorm ever witnessed, killing all who were exposed to it. This perturbed Pharaoh and he relented, and the storm stopped. But true to form, he changed his mind and got a plague of locusts for his trouble. They invaded the land and ate everything they could, like a school outing to McDonald's. But did he learn? No! So next, total darkness came over the land for three days. This seemed to be Pharaoh's last straw, but anger took hold of him and he sent Moses away, refusing to listen to him any more.

The last plague was the worst, the death of every first-born son in the land. The Israelites had to daub the blood of a lamb on their doorframes in order for this plague to skip them, or 'pass them over' – from which we get the name of the Passover festival. The Egyptians had had enough by now, despite their Pharaoh, and urged the Israelites to leave, even giving them parting gifts. This became the Exodus, the 'departure' of the Israelites from their Egyptian captivity.

Now you'd think that Pharaoh would have bitten the bullet, put it all down to experience and found some other unfortunates to press into service on his pyramids. But instead he jumped into his chariot and set off in pursuit of the Israelites, followed by every other chariot in Egypt, to 'head them off at the pass'. Our story ends with the parting of the Red Sea and the drowning of the whole Egyptian army, including the stubborn monarch.

Our second tyrant lived in Persia about 2,500 years ago. In the Book of Esther we read how King Ahasuerus of the Persian Empire got rid of his wife for answering him back once too often and installed the lovely Esther as queen in her place. Despite her craving for gefilte fish and her Barbra Streisand record collection (unconfirmed reports), he was unaware of her Jewish background. He was also unaware of the presence of her relative Mordechai, whom she regularly visited, until Mordechai had a stroke of luck (or divine favour?). One day he was sitting on his favourite chair by the city gate, minding his own business, when he accidentally overheard a plot to kill the king. Being a shrewd man, he figured that he could help himself if he handled the situation carefully, so he told the king and the plot was thwarted. In this way Mordechai gained favour with the king.

All seemed well for the moment, and the Jews of the day could sleep well at night (apart from the insomniacs) . . . but not for long, because this is when Haman came onto the scene. A descendant of the ancient Amalekites, old enemies of the Israelites, he managed to worm his way through the ranks until he became the chief minister to the king. Now this man was a severe egomaniac who demanded that all court officials regularly kneel down in honour of him. They all did this, except one: Mordechai. Mordechai, being a good Jew, refused to bow to any man as, according to the Law of Moses, this was idolatry (though he also had chronic rheumatism of the knee, but that's another story). Haman was enraged at this and, on finding out that Mordechai was Jewish, tricked the king into ordering not just the death of Mordechai, but the death of every Jew in the kingdom. They then drew lots (they cast the *pur*, from which comes the name *Purim*, the festival that commemorates these events), to find out on what day to execute this dastardly deed. Thanks to the bravery of Esther, this plot was thwarted and Haman and his ten sons were hanged on the very gallows he had made especially for Mordechai. These gallows were seventy-five feet high, which seems a little excessive to me. I thought Jews were meant to be stiff-necked, not long-necked! It seems that Haman wasn't the only one who hated the Jews, as thousands of others were waiting for the edict to do away with the Jews. This edict never came, but the tables were turned and their own 'death warrants' were sent to the Jews, who cheerfully obliged by annihilating them.

Now Haman was a true anti-Semite. Why kill just the one Jew who crossed you when you've got the power to destroy the whole nation of them? This was to become the motif for true anti-Semites through history, and Haman set the pattern for people such as Hitler in later years. For the Jews, *Purim* is in fact the most joyous day in the calendar, and Jews to this day commemorate the death of Haman by eating him, something that Jews are rather expert at (eating, that is, not eating people!). Little did this twisted man know that he would be remembered through the ages as a triangular pastry filled with poppy seeds, called *Hamantaschen*.

Returning to our story, it's time for a good hard look at anti-Semitism to see if we can get a handle on it. Historians admit that it is the longest and deepest hatred of human history. There have, of course, been many other hatreds, but none can compare with a hatred against a single people group that has lasted well over two thousand years and shows no sign of abating. Interestingly, in one context it has changed names – to the politically correct *anti-Zionism*. In some (usually left-wing) circles this is acceptable and we can even find some politically active Jews subscribing to this view. Self-hating Jews, no less, if only they knew it. Don't be fooled for a minute; it's just a new expression of an old hatred. Granted, there may be elements of inequality and injustice in the Palestinian situation in the Middle East, but there's far worse raging in every corner of the globe! Yet we don't coin a phrase to describe our position on these issues, do we? In drawing rooms and dinner parties across Britain, misled folk can openly declare themselves anti-Zionists and still have best friends who are Jewish. Attacking Israel on any level is just a comfortable and acceptable way of venting one's anti-Semitism.

So how do we explain this ancient hatred? Many have tried.

There has been the *sociological* angle, according to which the Jews were always an alien minority with a distinctive culture of their own, out of harmony with the culture of the surrounding Gentile nations. If this were true, the formation of the State of Israel would have removed anti-Semitism, which it clearly hasn't.

Then there's the *economic* angle, according to which the Jews have been accused of taking away jobs and money from Christians. This derives from the medieval insistence that moneylending was the only occupation a Jew was fit for. You could hardly blame the Jews for the fact that out of this restriction came great skills in international trade and finance and that Jews are found in positions of power and wealth all over the world. This provokes jealousy from others, leading to hatred.

Then there's the *ethnic* angle, whereby the Jews are believed to be a separate race, an inherently inferior one that is bent on polluting and corrupting the other inherently superior races. Character traits that have been attributed to the Jew to fuel anti-Semitism include the world-conqueror, the coward, the money-grabber, the show-off, the rootless wanderer ('Wandering Jew'), the heartless capitalist, the corrupter. These images were often the subject of popular cartoons in the nineteenth century in Europe, particularly in Germany. This was a key tenet of Nazism and we can see where that led.

Then there's the *political* angle, as mentioned earlier. Anti-Zionism is a key component of Arab and Muslim anti-Semitism, a reaction to the presence of the tiny Jewish state of Israel on 'Muslim' land.

Then there are the *conspiracy* theories. The Jews (Zionists) are bent on world domination. This is the *Zionist conspiracy* and is much loved by neo-Nazis and fundamentalist Muslim groups. A key mantra of these folk is *Holocaust revisionism*, by which they mean that part of this conspiracy is a complete fabrication of the facts of the Holocaust, i.e. they state that the Nazi Holocaust never really happened. Others on the lunatic fringe have stated that communism is also a Jewish conspiracy, though these people have gone quiet since the collapse of the Soviet Union.

The explanation that is most popular, for obvious reasons, among anti-Semites is the one that puts the blame fairly and squarely at the feet of the Jews themselves. It's because they choose isolation and a solitary existence for selfish, exclusive reasons, the reasoning goes. These people continue to berate the Jews for their stubborn regard for their *Torah* and for refusing to kow-tow to any other laws, arguing that this behaviour encourages the hatred of others. It's a reason of sorts, but it speaks more negatively about these other nations than about the Jews themselves, if their only sin is to live according to the laws that God gave them.

Then there's the *religious* angle, mentioned earlier. The Jews killed Christ, so it's up to us to wreak God's vengeance on these cursed people.

In Greek mythology there was a creature called the *Hydra*. It was a water serpent and it had many heads. When a head was cut off, two new heads appeared. Anti-Semitism, too, as we have seen, is many-headed and every new generation seems to be able to add a freshness to this ancient hatred. Yet there was a way of killing the Hydra, and later in this book we will discuss the identity of the

Hydra of anti-Semitism and how we can, like the Greek hero Hercules, find a way through its defences.

Orthodox Jews themselves see it in biblical terms. The *Midrash* refers to the Book of Malachi, where God says, *'I have loved Jacob, but Esau I have hated'* (Mal. 1:2–3). From this comes the observation, *'It is a well known principle that Esau hates Jacob'*, and from this they equate Esau with the whole Gentile world, saying in essence that anti-Semitism is a law, a mysterious principle laid down by God in His wisdom! So the idea is that rather than question the wisdom of God in this issue, they should seek to find ways of living with it. It's a sad conclusion, but it's the only rational way they could look at it, within their worldview.

We end on a sombre note because in the next chapter we are going to witness a moment in time when all the historical justifications for anti-Semitism came together in one place and raged unchecked for over a decade.

We have learnt that . . .
Anti-Semitism is a hatred that has lasted longer than any others and is still with us today, particularly in Europe. Many possible causes have been put forward, but none of them alone offers a satisfactory explanation.

Chapter 10

Jude!

This chapter is a climax to all the negative stuff that has gone before in our story. After this it gets a lot easier. But this is an important chapter because it represents a culmination and a fulfilment of all the dirt, grime and filth of anti-Semitism and acts as a warning klaxon alerting us to what can happen when pure evil is allowed to flow unchecked.

In 1942, at the height of the Second World War, a German reserve police battalion from Hamburg was given the mission of rounding up and massacring over 38,000 Jews in a village in Poland. The average age of these Germans was 39; they were middle class and most had no particular hatred of Jews. About a dozen out of the 500 refused to take part, and some more refused to carry on once the shooting had started, but the majority got on with it. Later on, some actually developed a taste for the job and volunteered to take part in other death squads. They had acquired a taste for killing and it didn't concern them.

One of them said this:

*'It was possible for me to shoot just the children. It so happened
that the mothers led the children by the hand. My neighbour shot
the mother and I shot the child, because I reasoned that the child
couldn't live without its mother. This soothed my conscience.'*

They were just following orders. As one man later
admitted, it was not until years later that he began to
consider that what he had done had not been right. He
had not given it a thought at the time.

I thought that I would start with this unsavoury episode
because rather than absolving the indescribably evil Nazi
leaders, it demonstrates that evil, to the extent of taking
human lives without conscience, is contagious. This story,
taken from the book *Ordinary Men*,[1] demonstrates just
how many of the Jews who died in the Nazi Holocaust
were killed at the hands of ordinary men.

But first, the facts in a nutshell. The Holocaust was the
systematic, bureaucratic annihilation of at least six million
Jews by the German Nazi regime and their collaborators
as state policy during the Second World War. In 1933,
approximately nine million Jews lived in the countries of
Europe that would be occupied by Germany during the
war. By 1945, two out of every three European Jews had
been killed. Although Jews were the primary victims,
other Nazi targets included Gypsies, the mentally or
physically disabled, Slavs, homosexuals and political and
religious dissidents.

To understand how the Holocaust could happen in a
country known for its sophistication and civilisation, we
need to explore some history.

Anti-Semitism had found fertile soil in the nineteenth
century, in Germany. The Nazis may have provided
practical 'solutions', but all the groundwork and theory
had been laid in the previous century. German
philosophers such as Ghillany, Arndt and Jahn were

producing work which took a most venomous stance towards the Jews. Ludwig Feuerbach said, *'Eating is the most solemn act or the initiation of the Jewish religion.'* (Some truth in that!) He continued, *'When the seventy elders ascended the mountain with Moses, "they saw God . . . they ate and they drank."'* (Yes, this is OK; it's what it says in the Bible.) But then he concluded, *'Thus with them what the sight of the Supreme Being heightened was the appetite for food.'*[2] This is contempt for Judaism, just a small step from full-blown anti-Semitism.

German philosophers and scientists now confounded all logic and began to put forward strange new theories about racial origins. It was summed up in the phrase *'purity of the blood'*. These people considered themselves of the Aryan race, a people originating in India. They even put forward the idea that Adam and Eve in the Garden of Eden only spoke German to each other! Well, anyway, this Aryan race was superior to all others, the race to conquer all before them. The problem is that in their long history they were in constant battle with the inferior . . . the sub-human . . . the evil Jew! Yes, the sub-human, inferior and tainted Jewish chosen race always seemed to thwart the intentions and destiny of the superior Aryan master race.

In 1899, Houston Stewart Chamberlain put all these myths together in a book called *Foundations of the Nineteenth Century*. It was a 1,500-page book packed with attacks on the Jews, such as *'The Jewish race is altogether bastardised, and its existence is a crime against the holy laws of life.'* This book sold almost one million copies: almost a million hearts willing to be diseased by lies and hatred. One could also imagine thousands of young German hearts and consciences anaesthetised in advance against the horrors of the Holocaust, forty years later.

Chamberlain wasn't the only anti-Semite in his family. His father-in-law was Richard Wagner, Hitler's favourite composer. Wagner, whether composing music or writing books, dedicated his life to anti-Semitism. It became a driving obsession and in 1881 he wrote this to the King of Bavaria:

> *'I regard the Jewish race as the born enemy of pure humanity and everything that is noble in it; it is certain that we Germans will go under before them, and perhaps I am the last German who knows how to stand up as an art-loving man against the Judaism that is already getting control of everything.'*

So the scene was set for Hitler and his wickedness.

What can I add to the millions of words written and tears shed on this subject? The German state became a diseased organ, poisoned by the virus of anti-Semitism, an irrational disease that inflames the mind while deadening the conscience. The Germans, whether you wish to believe it or not, were one of the most cultured, civilised societies at the turn of the twentieth century. Yet a few decades later these people were engaged in, or supporting, or turning a blind eye to, the most inhuman, evil activities ever conceived in the human mind. But consider this. If Haman, or the Inquisition, or the medieval state church had had the twentieth century's transportation systems or technologies of death and destruction, wouldn't they have done the same? The ultimate aim of anti-Semitism is not simply hatred of the Jews, but the *extinction* of the Jews. Wouldn't earlier anti-Semites, who also considered Jews to be inferior, sub-human or demonic, have chosen the same 'solution', rather than the 'inconvenience' of conversion, pogrom or deportation? We'll never know; we can only guess.

We can get a flavour of the mindless hatred that drove these Nazis by considering that so much energy, enthusiasm and – most importantly – material and human resources were expended by Nazi Germany in their attempted extermination of the Jews that there is every possibility they could have won the war if these resources had been diverted towards the war effort.

There are many individual stories that work together to make up the Holocaust: six million of them in fact. Each story tears at the heart and begs to be told, demands to be remembered. Yet we can't do them justice, just as these victims suffered without justice. So there will be no stories and no statistics. This sad story has been extensively documented in so many other places.

But before we pour out our righteous indignation against the Germans, what about the world community at large? In 1938, just before the start of the Second World War, there was a conference in Evian, France, called by the US President and attended by thirty-two nations with the objective of discussing the future of the European Jews. The Jews at that time were still free to move, but it was clear to many right-minded people that by staying within the clutches of the Nazi state they were putting themselves in great danger. So these delegates sat round a table and asked each other, *'Who's going to take in these Jews to save them from this fate?'* Do you know the outcome of this conference? Out of the millions of Jews in central Europe, the danger zone, only a few thousand were accommodated by these nations. One by one they all gave reasons why they couldn't take Jewish refugees – they would have loved to take them, but their hands were tied. Golda Meir, the future Israeli leader, was there. She commented:

'I don't think that anyone who didn't live through it can understand what I felt at Evian – a mixture of sorrow, rage, frustration and horror. I wanted to get up and scream at them all, "Don't you know that these numbers are human beings,

> *people who may spend the rest of their lives in concentration*
> *camps, or wandering around the world like lepers, if you don't*
> *let them in?"'*

Hitler saw the report of this conference and saw this
indifference as the all-clear for him to start the next stage
of his master plan. Four months later came *Kristallnacht*,
the 'night of the broken glass', when the word *Jude* (Jew)
sprayed on your shop front meant nothing less than a
death sentence. It was the first major step of the Final
Solution against the Jews.

The horrors of the Holocaust must never be forgotten,
and there's simply no space here to adequately get this
idea across. Instead I urge you to visit the Holocaust
experience at the Imperial War Museum in London, or
Yad Vashem in Israel, or one of the Holocaust museums in
the USA. You need to hear the testimonies of the
survivors, watch the Nazi propaganda films, see the
evocative exhibits.[3]

> *'I believe in the sun even when it is not shining.*
> *I believe in love even when not feeling it.*
> *I believe in God even when he is silent.'*

This short poem was found on a wall in a cellar in
Cologne, Germany, where Jews had hidden from the
Nazis but had ultimately perished. It speaks of a
spirituality that has been severely challenged by horrific
events. Many lost faith; others clung on regardless. Jews
cried out in utter anguish, but their Creator did not seem
to hear. Jews prayed and there was no response. Jews died
Kiddush HaShem, sanctifying the name of the Lord with
their last breath on earth, and the heavens responded with
a deafening silence.

How could the Jews continue to believe in a God who

allowed Auschwitz to happen? It's not humanly reasonable to do so; it's like a rejection by a loved one. There is a sense in saying, *'OK, you've let me down once too often, now leave me be to live the rest of my life in peace.'* Who could blame those Jews, particularly Holocaust survivors, who did so? Many did, and have allowed the experiences of the Holocaust to dictate the rest of their days on earth. Others have been set free by the power of God.

One thing we must remind ourselves of is the fact that God views individual Jews differently to the Jewish nation as a whole. As individuals, there is neither Jew nor Greek, slave nor free; the Jew competes on a level playing field, so to speak. For each and every Jew who has ever lived, God offers a personal relationship on a one-to-one basis. The trouble is that as a result of the actions of others, many of whom should have known better, the knowledge of this possibility was mostly kept from the Jewish people. On the other hand, on a national level, the Jews are a covenant people. As such they have responsibilities, leading to advantages or setbacks or, putting it more bluntly, blessings or curses.

On an individual basis, God is forever holding out His arms to us, whatever dire situation may surround us, whatever plans evil men and women may have for us. God's Word is clear on this. He will always show compassion for the weak and the defenceless, but the fate of these wicked is sealed and you can be assured that the Nazi perpetrators' eventual fate would be far worse than that of their victims. Let us read Psalm 9.

'I will praise you, O LORD, with all my heart; I will tell of all your wonders. I will be glad and rejoice in you; I will sing praise to your name, O Most High. My enemies turn back; they stumble and perish before you. For you have upheld my right and my cause; you have sat on your throne, judging righteously.

> *You have rebuked the nations and destroyed the wicked; you have blotted out their name for ever and ever. Endless ruin has overtaken the enemy, you have uprooted their cities; even the memory of them has perished. The LORD reigns for ever; he has established his throne for judgment. He will judge the world in righteousness; he will govern the peoples with justice. The LORD is a refuge for the oppressed, a stronghold in times of trouble. Those who know your name will trust in you, for you, LORD, have never forsaken those who seek you. Sing praises to the LORD, enthroned in Zion; proclaim among the nations what he has done. For he who avenges blood remembers; he does not ignore the cry of the afflicted. O LORD, see how my enemies persecute me! Have mercy and lift me up from the gates of death, that I may declare your praises in the gates of the Daughter of Zion and there rejoice in your salvation. The nations have fallen into the pit they have dug; their feet are caught in the net they have hidden. The LORD is known by his justice; the wicked are ensnared by the work of their hands. The wicked return to the grave, all the nations that forget God. But the needy will not always be forgotten, nor the hope of the afflicted ever perish. Arise, O LORD, let not man triumph; let the nations be judged in your presence. Strike them with terror, O LORD; let the nations know they are but men.'*

This may have been little consolation for those facing terrors at the hands of men and women without compassion, mercy or conscience, but the fact remains that in terms of life everlasting, God will provide a refuge for the oppressed; but for the oppressor – unless there are acts of sincere repentance and restitution (and very few of these have been documented) – no mercy will be shown. The Holocaust showed what human beings are capable of, but in the final judgement that no one will escape, all will see what God is capable of.

The Holocaust, as mentioned earlier, showed us what

happens when evil is allowed to go unchecked and every hatred of the human heart is given free rein. It proved the failure of humankind, not the failure of God. He gave humanity free will, and what the world witnessed in the 1940s was how low we can sink when we forsake morality and conscience. The Holocaust showed us that without God and His teachings, the earth could not survive; we would just end up killing each other.

If you wish to read more on the subject of God and the Holocaust, may I recommend that you read Chapter 13, 'Can theology survive after Auschwitz?' in Fred Wright's excellent book *Father, Forgive Us*.

Many Nazis were Roman Catholics or members of the state Protestant church but, since both church history and secular scientists were telling them that Jews were sub-human, haters of God and worthy of death, they allowed themselves to be instruments of this age-old hatred and killed Jews without a glimmer of conscience or thought of personal consequence. Hitler wrote in *Mein Kampf*, *'I am convinced that I am acting as the agent of our Creator. By fighting off the Jews, I am doing the Lord's work.'* The attempted annihilation of the Jews was carried out by these twisted hearts with religious zeal, a zeal nurtured by years of anti-Semitism infiltrated into the German church and the German soul.

As mentioned in Chapter 3, the Jewish people were in *Galut*, in exile. It was a natural consequence of the warnings in Deuteronomy 28. During this exile, it was as if God left them in the hands of man, just as in the final hours of Jesus' own life he was placed in the hands of man. An implication of this is that outside Israel, the Promised Land, life for the Jew was always going to be precarious. This puts an added emphasis on the true nature of *Galut*. One of the major consequences of the Holocaust was to signal the death-throes of the exile, in the miraculous provision of the State of Israel, a land to provide for the first time in 1,900 years a safe haven for Jewish people. It's my belief that God, His tender heart grieved to the utmost by the frenzy of evil deeds against His people in the Holocaust and overwhelmed by the sheer number of devout Jews going to their death *Kiddush HaShem*, simply said, '*Enough is enough; I cannot leave my beloved people any longer at the mercy of the Gentile nations. It is time for their homecoming.*'

Once installed in the land of Israel, although anti-Semitism was never going to leave them alone (taking a new form in Arab Muslim hatred), they would be masters of their own destiny in their own land, with their first self-governance since the time of the kings of Judah. This is the importance of Israel to the Jewish people. Most of us, living in material comfort and perceived safety in the west, have yet to realise this. Perhaps the coming days will show us otherwise, as happened with the Jews of Poland and Germany, who also thought in the mid-tweneith century that they were safely integrated into these countries.

As a footnote to this sorry episode I finish with a poem written by 12-year-old Eva Pickova in a Jewish ghetto; she died two years later in Auschwitz.

Fear

Today the ghetto knows a different fear,
Close in its grip, Death wields an icy scythe.
An evil sickness spreads a terror in its wake.
The victims of its shadow weep and writhe.
Today a father's heartbeat tells his fright
And mothers bend their heads into their hands.
Now children choke and die with typhus here,
A bitter tax is taken from their bands.
My heart still beats inside my breast
While friends depart for other worlds.

Perhaps it's better – who can say –
Than watching this, to die today?
No, no, my God we want to live!
Not watch our numbers melt away.
We want to have a better world,
We want to work – we must not die![4]

Near the head of this chapter we heard of those 'ordinary men', ordinary Germans who were turned into killing machines, agents of the evil Nazi regime in the Final Solution. Yet before the war these were regular people like you and me. This speaks volumes about the evil that lurks within all our hearts and the ease with which anti-Semitism can find fertile soil for its propagation. We must all be so watchful.

We have learnt that . . .
The Holocaust was the ultimate expression of anti-Semitism, showing what can happen if the evil that is in the human heart goes unchecked. Those who perpetrated it will have to answer for it one day, as it says in Psalm 9: *'For he who avenges blood remembers; he does not ignore the cry of the afflicted.'*

NOTES

1 Browning, Christopher, *Ordinary Men: Reserve Police Battalion 101 and the Final Solution in Poland* (Perennial, 1993).
2 Feuerbach, Ludwig, *Essence of Christianity*, Pt 1, ch. 11 (1841)
3 You can visit on-line exhibitions on the Holocaust referenced at http://www.yad-vashem.org.il/exhibitions/index_exhibitions.html
4 The original manuscript for this poem can be found in the Jewish Museum, Prague.

Chapter 11

Natural Branches

There is an important statement I must make. It is so important that I am going to write it in CAPITAL LETTERS. It's simple, obvious to some, but others continue to get it wrong and allow it to influence their thoughts, attitudes and behaviour towards Jewish people. The statement is this: INDIVIDUAL JEWISH PEOPLE ARE NOT SAVED UNLESS THEY ACCEPT JESUS AS THEIR MESSIAH. It has to be stated clearly and explicitly, as so many people get it wrong. Jews in the world, whether in the UK, the USA or even in Israel, are as dead in their sins as those who surround them unless they have made a sincere commitment to their Jewish Saviour, who came to the world two thousand years ago to save them and who still reaches out to them with outstretched arms, saying, *'These arms are getting tired now, but they're still waiting for you.'*

Christians who express a love of Israel and the Jewish people have to examine their motivation honestly and sincerely on this matter. Christian Zionists are people who have seen the sorry history of the treatment of the Jews by Christians in the past and have woken to these errors, seeking to fight against anti-Semitism and to affirm Jewish people and their biblical rights to the Land of Israel. But there can be a danger of going too far here, highlighted lucidly by Kay of AMITI (Artists Musicians Israelis Together for Integrity) in her paper, *An exposé of favourable discrimination towards Jewish people within Christian Zionism, and its subsequent effect upon Jewish-Gentile relations*.

She goes as far as to say, 'Those very same Christians who *seek to fight discrimination against the Jewish people are now in danger of ignorantly perpetuating it.'* She justifies her comment by examining how some Christians are also exercising discrimination, albeit a positive one, in blind support of Israel and the Jewish people. If this is on the basis of God's promises to the Jewish *people*, then it puts added expectations on relationships with *individual* Jews, elevating them to some perceived and unrealistic super-spiritual role that is simply not true.

It is true that, as discussed in Chapter 8, there have been some remarkable achievements by individual Jews over the last few centuries and there is a mysterious aspect to this, but the assertion by Shylock, in Shakespeare's *Merchant of Venice*, works both ways: *'If you prick us, do we not bleed? If you tickle us, do we not laugh? If you poison us, do we not die?'* God sees individual Jews and Gentiles as equals; there is no personal favouritism for the Jew. That's the point of the verse in Galatians, *'There is neither Jew nor Greek, slave nor free, male nor female, for you are all one in Christ Jesus'* (Gal. 3:28).

We must learn to distinguish between Jewish people and a Jewish *person*. God's covenants with Abraham, Moses and David are for the Jewish people as a whole, the Jewish nation, wherever it may be in the world. These covenants speak of big things, important things. They tell us that a Saviour was to come from the seed of a given people, that these people will inherit the land now known (by most of us) as Israel and that these people are going to have a hard time of it until they return to this land. These people are the Jewish people. Individual Jews have no relationship with the Saviour, except through faith. Not every Jew (I believe) is automatically going to migrate to Israel, though all are urged to. Individual Jews have only had a hard time of it in history if they have lived demonstrably as members of the Jewish race. Many have become assimilated – living as non-Jews – and escaped persecution, pogroms and the death camps. Individual Jews have free will to accept or reject Jesus as their Messiah. But not so the Jewish nation. It has a God-given destiny, in fact a glorious one, from which it can never escape.

Look at an army of ants. Here they go, shifting twigs, leaves and food along a conveyor belt of individual worker ants. Toiling as a group, often numbered in the thousands, they corporately achieve great things, though the individual effort of each ant is minimal. When disaster strikes, whether it be a sudden downpour or the intervention of a human child, their goal can be thwarted, an ant hill destroyed or a production line disrupted. This is a disaster for the whole group, not necessarily for an individual ant, which could have survived to live another day. Picture a single ant, like 'Z' in the animated film *Antz*. He had free will. He was free to woo the princess and do his own thing. (Interestingly, this character was voiced by an archetypal modern Jew, Woody Allen.) When disaster comes, he can always hide or run away. It's not a complete picture and may not necessarily help you to understand the Jewish people, but it's the best I can come up with.

It seems that when a Jew becomes a believer in Jesus he or she enters not only into a new life but also into a new debate. Apparently it is not enough for a Jew simply to take on the name of Christian like any other new believer and be done with it. New Jewish believers find themselves deluged with labels. They may find themselves called a Hebrew Christian, a Messianic Jew, a Completed Jew or a Jewish believer, but only rarely a common-or-garden Christian. You don't see Hindu Christians or Messianic Muslims, so why burden the Jews with labels? Why can't they just merge into the background and humbly accept their new station as part of the 'Body of Messiah' as a new creation?

Some Gentile Christians may shrug their shoulders and say, *'Just like the Jews: they still think they're specially chosen. Why can't they just be like us?'* Yet it is often Gentiles who treat us differently to start with. In my experience it is rare to find a Gentile Christian who is indifferent to my background. From just plain curiosity to a vague respect born out of the 'blessed is he who blesses' view of the Jew, we always manage to evoke some sort of response. Although I initially found it quietly humorous and touching to be consulted on all things Hebrew and Jewish (if only they knew that my knowledge and training stopped on the afternoon of my bar mitzvah), it can be a bit wearing after a time.

But it's not all the fault of Gentiles. We Jews are a proud people and are not exactly reticent when nudged onto a pedestal. Perhaps we see it as recompense for two thousand years of persecution: it makes a welcome change to be lifted up in honour rather than struck down in hatred. The question we really need to address as Jewish believers in Jesus is: How does God see us? Does He see us any differently from the way He sees other believers? Of course not, as I said earlier, but I will repeat it anyway.

On an individual basis, in terms of our personal salvation we are no different to, and no better than, any other component of the 'Body of Messiah'. (*'There is neither*

Jew nor Greek', Gal. 3:28.) Jews are not saved through Judaism, but through Jesus, like everyone else. (*'Salvation is found in no one else, for there is no other name under heaven given to men by which we must be saved'*, Acts 4:12.)

On a national level, as the 'remnant of Israel' (i.e. Jews who believe in Jesus, the Jewish Messiah), we have a different responsibility, towards our natural family (unsaved Jews) and our spiritual family (fellow believers, Jew and Gentile). To our unsaved Jewish family our responsibility is to give a priority to their salvation ('. . . *first for the Jew'*, Rom. 1:16). To our spiritual family our responsibility is to help to restore the balance that has been lost to the church as a result of over 1,500 years of Gentile domination. However little we can contribute to this, I am increasingly aware of the duty of Jewish believers to spend time studying our roots and culture so that we can feed a church that is becoming increasingly hungry for such nourishment.

The only covenant that is currently in operation for individual Jews is the New Covenant. It is clearly stated as a prophecy in Jeremiah 31:31–33:

> *'"The time is coming," declares the LORD, "when I will make a new covenant with the house of Israel and with the house of Judah. It will not be like the covenant I made with their forefathers when I took them by the hand to lead them out of Egypt, because they broke my covenant, though I was a husband to them," declares the LORD. "This is the covenant that I will make with the house of Israel after that time," declares the LORD. "I will put my law in their minds and write it on their hearts. I will be their God, and they will be my people."'*

The covenant was kick-started through the life and death of Jesus of Nazareth. Just like the ones with Abraham, Moses and David, it was a covenant with the Jewish people. Jesus came, first, for his own people, the Jews. How do we know this? Well, he spoke of it himself:

> *'These twelve Jesus sent out with the following instructions: "Do not go among the Gentiles or enter any town of the Samaritans. Go rather to the lost sheep of Israel"' (Mt. 10:5–6).*

Paul, the dominant writer of the New Testament, also wrote of it:

> *'I am not ashamed of the gospel, because it is the power of God for the salvation of everyone who believes: **first for the Jew**, then for the Gentile' (Rom. 1:16, my emphasis).*

It makes sense really. The Jews were God's people, the keeper of His covenants and His scriptures (i.e. the Bible). They may have wandered away from the centre of God's will, but they were God's best chance, at that time, for a people of His *New* Covenant. Just look at the alternatives – Greeks, Romans and others, thoroughly immersed in a pagan culture and religious system. He could hardly use *them* to get things going. The Jews had a head start – two thousand years of it! It doesn't need the mind of a genius to understand why God was going to get the new deal going with the Jews first (those who were willing to listen).

Paul sets the scene quite adequately in Romans 9:4–5:

> *'Theirs is the adoption as sons; theirs the divine glory, the covenants, the receiving of the law, the temple worship and the promises. Theirs are the patriarchs, and from them is traced the human ancestry of Christ, who is God over all, for ever praised!'*

The raw material had been nursed and developed over two thousand years of turbulent history. It was time for God to redeem His investment.

And many Jews did accept the new deal, at the start. All Jesus' disciples were Jews, as were the first new believers, all three thousand of them on the first Day of Pentecost in Jerusalem, when the church was born.

But what came next was totally unexpected, to the Jews at least. After all, they'd had God to themselves since He first beckoned Abraham out of the eastern lands. But it couldn't last. Could they really believe that God would only be interested in one tiny nation and would be happy for the rest to go (literally) to hell? Didn't they realise that they, the Jewish nation, were simply God's chosen instrument to establish a bridgehead among the nations? Does a trowel complain when the builder uses it to create a house?

God gave a clue at the beginning of the story.

> *'The* LORD *had said to Abram, "Leave your country, your people and your father's household and go to the land I will show you. I will make you into a great nation and I will bless you; I will make your name great, and you will be a blessing. I will bless those who bless you, and whoever curses you I will curse; and all peoples on earth will be blessed through you' (Gen. 12:1–3).*

All peoples on earth were going to be blessed here, not just a favoured few. It was a theme repeated by the great Old Testament prophet, Isaiah.

> *'And now the* LORD *says – he who formed me in the womb to be his servant to bring Jacob back to him and gather Israel to himself, for I am honoured in the eyes of the* LORD *and my God has been my strength – he says: "It is too small a thing for you to be my servant to restore the tribes of Jacob and bring back those of Israel I have kept. I will also make you a light for the Gentiles, that you may bring my salvation to the ends of the earth"' (Is. 49:5–6).*

Of course it was too small a thing. We're talking of heaven and hell here!

> '*All the nations you have made* will come and worship before you, O Lord; they will bring glory to your name' (Ps. 86:9, my emphasis).

The nations could hardly give glory to God if they didn't know Him. So they had to get to know Him first. Jews weren't natural evangelists, particularly to the hated Gentiles, who had never done them any favours. Remember the story of Jonah and his distaste for preaching to the Gentile city of Nineveh? '*How could God be so merciful to such a wicked city?*' cried Jonah. '*How could God be so merciful to such a wicked people?*' cried Jesus' chief disciple, Simon Peter, until God gave him a dream to change his mind and sent him to Cornelius, the Gentile Centurion.

> 'Then Peter began to speak: "I now realise how true it is that God does not show favouritism but accepts men *from every nation who fear him* and do what is right"' (Acts 10:34–35, my emphasis).

The scene was set for the explosion of the Gospel of Jesus, from Jerusalem to Judea and Samaria and to the ends of the earth, a process that is still in full flow today.

So the Gentiles were allowed in, but they were never intended to dominate. The ideal situation, of Jew and Gentile in balance, is described by Paul in the letter to the Ephesians:

> 'Therefore, remember that formerly you who are Gentiles by birth and called "uncircumcised" by those who call themselves "the circumcision" (that done in the body by the hands of men) –

*remember that at that time you were separate from Christ,
excluded from citizenship in Israel and foreigners to the
covenants of the promise, without hope and without God in the
world. But now in Christ Jesus you who once were far away have
been brought near through the blood of Christ. For he himself is
our peace, who has made the two one and has destroyed the
barrier, the dividing wall of hostility, by abolishing in his flesh
the law with its commandments and regulations. His purpose
was to create in himself one new man out of the two, thus
making peace, and in this one body to reconcile both of them to
God through the cross, by which he put to death their hostility'
(Eph. 2:11–16).*

A bold ideal, but not one that has ever been achieved in
the Christian world (the Puritans tried it, but without a
single Jew in sight) – a Christianity where Jew and Gentile
live together in harmony and understanding, each
contributing towards the relationship, creating a shining
witness to the world of a people to be envied. Within a few
generations of the Gentiles being allowed in, they had
established total domination and stripped away the
Jewish roots of the faith, taking on in their place pagan
practices from the cultures of the world.

It was a tragedy, not just for the Jews but for the Gentiles
too. If only they had read and understood what Paul had
to say in his letter to the Romans, they might have
tempered their treatment of the Jewish people. Countless
Jews may have lost their lives during this period, but what
do you think was the condition of the souls of the
Christians who were at the forefront of the relentless anti-
Semitism? Paul explained it very clearly in his letter to the
Roman Gentile Christians.

He turns us all into gardeners. He tells us to imagine an
olive tree – not so easy for modern people, particularly in
the dodgy British climate. For the Jews at the time of Jesus

it was a tree of great importance, a source of much that was needed for daily living. It provided olives for eating and olive oil for use in cooking, as fuel for lamps, in medicine and as anointing oil. It may not have been pretty to look at, but it was a king among trees. The olive leaf and branch have been symbols of peace to this day, from the time of Noah's flood.

In Romans chapter 11, he helps us to get a grip on the relationship between Jews and Gentiles in the Body of Messiah. Cast your mind back to the early days of Abraham and, with your spiritual eyes, imagine God planting an olive seed and watching as the first shoots burst from the ground. Then, as Isaac and Jacob appear on the scene, a tiny young olive tree has appeared in the spiritual landscape. As the Messianic line unfolds from Judah through to David, branches thrust their way into the sky until, by the time we get to the days of Jesus, the tree is well established. It is starting to grow now at an alarming rate. Every new Jew born has a branch in this tree. Growth is satisfactory, until something strange happens. Branches are starting to fall to the ground. For every new branch that appears, seemingly another is broken away, falling to the ground.

Eventually, other branches appear in their place, but these are not branches growing out of the tree itself; instead they are fully grown branches taken from a wild olive tree, added to the tree in the gaps left by the broken branches. These grafted-in branches are added at a faster and faster pace until, before long, the upper branches of the olive tree are totally dominated by these unnatural additions. These wild olive branches may be contrary to nature, yet they still produce fruit. But the natural branches are few and far between.

Now that I've set the picture, read the scriptures, then return to the description above.

'If some of the branches have been broken off, and you, though a wild olive shoot, have been grafted in among the others and now share in the nourishing sap from the olive root, do not boast over those branches' (Rom. 11:17–18).

Up to the time of Jesus the olive tree clearly represents, in some way, the Jewish people. The tree itself seems to be the place of God's blessing and all the branches are Jewish. We can imagine that a massive pruning exercise must have taken place at the time of the exile of the Northern Kingdom of Israel, branches lopped off as the Jews of the northern tribes disappear into obscurity and outside God's purposes. But now, at the time of Paul's writings, he speaks of the branches that were falling to the ground, natural branches representing Jews who have rejected Jesus and consequently fall away from the place of blessing. Their place was (and still is) taken by Gentiles who have accepted Jesus as their Messiah. These are the wild olive shoots, grafted into the gaps and feeding from the tree, receiving the blessings. They are not the natural branches, so it's not a perfect fit, but they benefit nevertheless.

'. . . do not boast over those branches. If you do, consider this: You do not support the root, but the root supports you' (Rom. 11:18).

Paul warns the Gentiles, the wild olive branches, that they should be thankful for their status and should always be aware that theirs is a position of favour. The argument continues:

'You will say then, "Branches were broken off so that I could be grafted in"' (Rom. 11:19).

Branches were broken off because there were some Jews

who failed to believe in Jesus. Their position was taken by the Gentiles. Then comes a warning.

> *'Granted. But they were broken off because of unbelief, and you stand by faith. Do not be arrogant, but be afraid' (Rom. 11:20).*

Do not be arrogant, but be afraid is the warning. The reason is then given.

> *'For if God did not spare the natural branches, he will not spare you either. Consider therefore the kindness and sternness of God: sternness to those who fell, but kindness to you, provided that you continue in his kindness. Otherwise, you also will be cut off' (Rom. 11:21–22).*

Bearing in mind that faith is a gift of God, if He is seemingly so willing to abandon the natural branches, the Jews, how much more willing will He be to do the same for the unnatural ones?

> *'And if they do not persist in unbelief, they will be grafted in, for God is able to graft them in again' (Rom. 11:23).*

Some say the Jews are finished. Paul doesn't, and God certainly doesn't. He is willing and able to re-graft the Jews, the natural branches, into the olive tree, the place of blessing and salvation.

> *'After all, if you were cut out of an olive tree that is wild by nature, and contrary to nature were grafted into a cultivated olive tree, how much more readily will these, the natural branches, be grafted into their own olive tree!' (Rom. 11:24).*

Paul summarises his warning to the Gentiles who have been added to the tree in the place of Jews. He reminds them of their grace and favour and points out that the Jews, the natural branches, could be re-grafted as a much better fit into the olive tree.

> *'I do not want you to be ignorant of this mystery, brothers, so that you may not be conceited: Israel has experienced a hardening in part until the full number of the Gentiles has come in' (Rom. 11:25).*

It's all a mystery. But although none may know the mind of God, He wants us to appreciate the outworkings of this mystery. Again it's a warning to the Gentiles, to stop them getting puffed up and conceited. There is something very deep and mystical going on here. The Jews, through their persistent unbelief as a race, have suffered the same fate as Pharaoh at the time of Moses, as well as many others in biblical history. They have experienced a *hardening*. God has allowed their hearts to harden in their rejection of Jesus as Messiah, and the result of this is to allow those wild olive branches, the Gentiles, a place in the olive tree of blessing. The Jews as a whole (not all of them, as I and many others can personally testify) have rejected Messiah and this has allowed the Gentiles in. It's an awesome fact, but it is true, and what is often ignored is that a time is going to come when the full number of Gentiles has come in, and then God's favour is going to swing back to the Jews. And when that happens, well, read on.

> *'And so all Israel will be saved, as it is written: "The deliverer will come from Zion; he will turn godlessness away from Jacob"' (Rom. 11:26).*

This verse has been discussed and debated by the theological giants, so I won't enter that particular arena except to say that, to some degree, God is going to soften those hard hearts and the light of the Gospel is going to shine in places that have been closed to it for many generations.

And when that happens, the world will be transformed. Paul speaks of it earlier in that same chapter, just before his warning to the Gentiles. He is talking to them about the Jews here:

> *'Again I ask: Did they stumble so as to fall beyond recovery? Not at all! Rather, because of their transgression, salvation has come to the Gentiles to make Israel envious. But if their transgression means riches for the world, and their loss means riches for the Gentiles, how much greater riches will their fullness bring! I am talking to you Gentiles. Inasmuch as I am the apostle to the Gentiles, I make much of my ministry in the hope that I may somehow arouse my own people to envy and save some of them. For if their rejection is the reconciliation of the world, what will their acceptance be but life from the dead?' (Rom. 11:11–15).*

I will let the above passage speak for itself. It is further evidence of the future role of the Jewish people in God's plan; indeed, their future speaks of a glorious future for the whole world.

And can you imagine it? Look back at the list of Jewish movers and shakers in Chapter 8. Can you imagine what blessings could flow to the world from the coming to faith of such as Steven Spielberg, Michael Howard or Alan Sugar? Nothing less than *life from the dead*, as it says.

So, where are we now? We've just read of God's plan of salvation for the Gentiles and the role played in it by the Jewish people. Earlier we read of the balance that God intended, of a church with Jew and Gentile working together and worshipping together.

The church needs to find this balance as never before, but in any attempt to achieve this there are dangers for both Jewish and Gentile believers.

Jewish believers need to keep a tight rein on how far they go in this important task of helping to restore the balance. At the end of the day they are, as are all Christians, our Lord's representatives on earth. There's a danger that they may start 'believing the publicity' of those Christians who perhaps unintentionally place Jewish believers on a pedestal. One such pastor always jokes when he meets me of 'touching the hem of my garment' and receiving a blessing. Is it a joke, or is there something else there? We must not give in to pride. It's one thing to be proud of your heritage, but it's another to use this in order to feel superior to other, Gentile, believers. It's just not on, and it can do nothing but harm to this precarious balance we strive for. Of all the 'deadly sins', pride is said to be the most lethal, as it is the one that places us at the centre of everything and relegates God to a mere bit part in the scheme of things. We must continue to remind ourselves that God originally chose the Jews despite themselves, not because of a natural superiority. He chose them for no other reason than that it was them that He chose! So no boasting to the grafted-in branches!

The danger for Gentile believers, when they strive to restore this balance, is also to go too far. Messianic fellowships have been founded, where Jews and Gentiles meet together with an emphasis on a Hebraic expression of faith in the teaching, liturgy and worship. They tend still to be predominantly Gentile in the UK, with typically no more than 30 per cent of the membership being from a Jewish background. In areas with few Jews, I have heard of some such fellowships with not a single Jew in the congregation. One can respect and understand the needs and motivation behind such expressions of faith, but one can also sense the dangers. Imagine an unsaved Jew arriving at a Messianic fellowship with few (or no) Jews, where Hebrew songs are sung, Jewish festivals are celebrated and many of the prayers are based on the Jewish prayer book. Would this be a good witness to a Jew who is conscious of a history of persecution and hatred by the Christian world? His immediate reaction is to see the natural and horrific conclusion of seventeen centuries of Jewish persecution at the hands of Christians. *'They have stolen our possessions, our well-being and our lives, and now they steal our culture and heritage! Have they left us nothing?'* I have been to such fellowships, where Gentiles wear skullcaps and prayer shawls, speak Yiddish and declare in their testimony that Messianic Judaism (rather than Jesus) has saved them. I know this is an extreme case, but, to quote again a verse mentioned earlier, Gentiles, particularly those who profess to love the Jewish people, must realise that salvation has come to the Gentiles to make Israel envious. Are your actions in accordance with this command?

Gentile Christians who have studied the Jewish roots of their faith have been mightily enriched, particularly when they are able to teach others in their churches or worship with like-minded believers in Messianic fellowships. But – and this is a big but – unless there is a genuine and demonstrable love for the Jewish people, it is a selfish exercise, carried out just for personal blessing. It may bless you, but in no way is it blessing the Jewish people or providing a balance in our expressions of our faith. Sure, you can learn from the Jewish roots, but don't neglect the very people who literally shed their blood to ensure that these teachings have survived to enrich you. It's not rocket science. Just treat your Jewish neighbour first as a human being, and the Holy Spirit will do the rest.

Returning to the article by Kay, it is worth paying heed to her conclusion.

'We must learn to embrace the paradox, through making a

distinction between relationships with individual Jews and our views of the Jewish people as a whole. This will invite the God of Israel back onto centre stage and in doing so spur the Christian Zionist into the greatest expression of Biblical support for the Jewish people, first and foremost a Spirit-led relentless proclamation of the crucified and resurrected Jewish Messiah, the sole true hope and comfort of Zion. With the priority of salvation binding Jew and Gentile together, both will be able to stand in mutual depravity yet God-given dignity before the throne of Messiah. Only then will both be able to wonder in awe at the election of Israel; only then will the tension between God's fairness and His sovereign choices be truly understood.'

We have learnt that . . .
Jewish people need Jesus just as others do. Christianity must find a balance between its Jewish and Gentile elements. Gentiles must be aware of the grace and favour offered to them as grafts, replacing the Jewish natural branches, into the olive tree.

Epilogue

It's been a rough ride, hasn't it? It's been an incredible story, and in this case truth is surely stranger than fiction. One thing we can't do is wave our story away as a strange anomaly of history; we must look deeper than that. In fact, the whole saga begs us to answer two questions:

1 *How have the Jews managed to survive so long?* How many other people have a history that stretches back four thousand years? The Assyrians, still a distinct people after centuries of dispersion, are their only serious competition, though they are over a thousand years younger.

2 *Why have they been so hated by so many other people for so many different reasons?* Christ killers, Children of Satan, Child kidnappers, Conspirators of Zion, Capitalists, Communists – and that's just the Cs!

These questions are connected, though, and should be held in tension with each other. In fact, they can become one question, one urgent, anguished plea:

How have the Jews managed to survive so long despite being hated by so many people?

This can be seen to be one of the central mysteries of history, alongside the big ones (how did life begin?) and knocking the smaller ones (who shot JFK?) into a cocked hat. It's such a big question because it uncovers a drama that has been unfolding for thousands of years, but hidden to most. The drama is a classic conflict between good and evil, between two great powers that have been in opposition since time began.

If we concede this possibility, perhaps the evidence can start to make sense. We can see that the reason why the Jews have survived so long is that a great power has been protecting them, and the reason why they have been hated for so long is that another great power has been attacking them. This provides us with an answer to our key question.

The reason why the Jews have managed to survive so long despite being hated by so many people is that the power that is protecting them is *greater* than the power that has been attacking them. God against Satan, the devil. No contest.

The story is told of Frederick II of Prussia asking his doctor for a proof of the existence of God. The reply was immediate: *'The Jews, your majesty,'* replied the good doctor.

Why on earth should this be? Could the evidence we have presented be so smothered by the fingerprints of God that a forensic sceptic would have to be blinkered to ignore it? Can the story of the Jews really point us to God? Can you think of any other explanation? It is, in my estimation, one of the most powerful apologetics for the existence of God and not to be dismissed lightly, particularly now you have had time to examine the evidence of history in this book.

We can imagine King Fred posing a second question, asking the doctor for a proof of the existence of the devil. Equally immediately the answer could have come. *'Anti-Semitism, your majesty,'* would be the reply. *'Hatred of the Jews.'*

The question that we asked – how have the Jews managed to survive so long despite being hated by so many people? – cannot be answered by referring to the wisdom of historians, philosophers, psychologists, politicians or sociologists. They have all failed. There is only one solution, a spiritual one, but in our materialist way of peering at the world, it's probably the last thing we want to hear. It goes against the grain of our secular world-system, but that doesn't make it any less true.

The truth is so plain to see that we should be shouting it from the rooftops. There is an awesome, unseen battle going on for our hearts and minds. It's a battle that will continue long after we die and, indeed, the consequences of this battle affect all of us, regardless of whether we believe in God or the devil or whatever. At the end of your life you will be pitched into this battle whether you like it or not, whether you have lived your life as a committed Christian or as a committed atheist. Truth is truth, it's not all in the eye of the beholder; it's a solid, unchanging truth that is going to determine where you end up after death.

To help your understanding of why a loving God could allow the Holocaust, let's look at the situation from a different angle. God could have chosen to protect His chosen people through these turbulent times when anti-Semitism has ruled the roost. To counter the seeds of hatred planted in the hearts of men against the Jews by the devil, God could instead have put a supernatural love in the hearts of all Christians. But surely that would have taken away their free will (the devil has no problem with people's free will, he just wishes to dominate and influence souls in the best way he can). In the final analysis, we all have free will to make our own decisions, whether to accept Jesus as our Saviour or whether to love or hate God's chosen people, the Jews. The choice is yours – it's free, but there is ultimately a cost, so use it wisely.

Whether or not you consider the subject material of this book relevant to your lifestyle is not important. What is important is that the story of the Jews serves to help you realise that there's more to this world than what you can see, hear, smell or feel.

If you are Jewish, you must realise that your heart has been wrapped in chains and securely locked up for centuries. But there is a key to this lock. It has grown rusty and has been more commonly used as a weapon against you, but it is coming back into view. That key is Jesus of Nazareth. He is the key to understanding and the key to life. Be bold; you have nothing to lose. You will receive such knowledge, wisdom and understanding that you will regret you did not find him earlier. I certainly did.

In the words of Moses, *'This day I call heaven and earth as witnesses against you that I have set before you life and death, blessings and curses. Now choose life, so that you and your children may live'* (Deut. 30:19).

Choose life!

For Gentile Christians among you, given that I consider the only valid explanation to the questions posed is that there are spiritual forces afoot, what exactly do I mean? I will bow to the insights and knowledge of the late lamented Derek Prince to furnish an explanation. In his teaching letter (No. 7) on *The Root of Anti-Semitism*, he says this:

> *'While I was preaching in our local church in Jerusalem, quite unexpectedly I heard myself say, "Anti-Semitism can be summed up in one word – MESSIAH!!" At that moment I*

understood that from its beginning Anti-Semitism had one
source – Satan – who was motivated by the knowledge that the
One who was to be his conqueror, the Messiah, would come
through a people that would be specially prepared by God.'

He goes on to explain that the Jews, the people in
question, were targets of Satan through their history,
either through being enticed into idolatry (early history)
or through complete destruction (later history). The
reason for this hatred is that he knows that his days are
numbered, a countdown culminating in the return of
Jesus the Messiah. But this event won't happen until two
conditions are fulfilled.

Firstly, the Christian Gospel is to be preached to all
nations.

'And this gospel of the kingdom will be preached in the whole
world as a testimony to all nations, and then the end will come'
(Mt. 24:14).

Secondly, the Jews must be in place and in a position to
ask Jesus to return. In Matthew 23:38–39, Jesus said to the
Jews in Jerusalem, *'See, your house is left to you desolate. For*
I tell you, you will not see me again until you say, "Blessed is he
who comes in the name of the Lord."'

The Jews must be in place, in this final drama at the end
of all things, to ask Jesus to return. Who knows what the
circumstances will be, but they are likely to be fairly
extreme and desperate. Their hearts will be ready; the
hardening spoken of in the previous chapter will have
been broken down.

'And I will pour out on the house of David and the inhabitants of
Jerusalem a spirit of grace and supplication. They will look on
me, the one they have pierced, and they will mourn for him as

one mourns for an only child, and grieve bitterly for him as one
grieves for a first born son' (Zech. 12:10).

And when they do that, anti-Semitism will be no more, because the root cause of it will have been taken away. I pray that those Christians who have been hardened against Israel and the Jewish people don't have to wait until then to realise the truth of their errors.

'"Shout and be glad, O Daughter of Zion. For I am coming, and
I will live among you," declares the LORD. "Many nations will
be joined with the LORD in that day and will become my people. I
will live among you and you will know that the LORD Almighty
has sent me to you. The LORD will inherit Judah as his portion in
the holy land and will again choose Jerusalem"' (Zech. 2:10–12).

At that time God's scales of justice will take a sudden swing in favour of His people, the Jews. When that happens, all who have perpetrated anti-Semitism, who have acted against 'the apple of His eye', will be punished accordingly. By that time the Jews, who have been scattered to the four winds, will have returned to their land, Israel. In this future time God will live with His people, who will be taken from all nations. Yes, you hear me right – at this time it's not a case of us living in heaven with God, but rather of God coming down to earth and living with us.

The interesting verse is Zechariah 10:12, which gives a pretty good description of God's view of the future and the land of Israel. Here God explicitly states that Judah (the southern part of Israel), and in particular Jerusalem, will be where He chooses to live in this future time, not London or New York or Paris. And the people He chooses to live with will be taken from the Jews, the apple of His eye, along with all others from the nations (Gentiles) who have been 'granted membership' of the fellowship of believers. So, be warned. Seek blessing, not judgement, by aligning yourself with God's purposes towards His ancient and modern people, the Jews.

Church history, as I've said before, tells a sorry story. Imagine you are in an ocean and you witness the birth of a great wave. From small beginnings, perhaps a few ripples, it builds up and gathers momentum, sweeping along all that it finds in its path. Such is the tide of church history. The early ripples were the first seeds of the faith, representing its truest expression as its followers honestly lived out the words of its founder. Yet as it built up, it gathered to itself other waves that were around, other worldviews and philosophies. It absorbed Greek philosophy, paganism, greed and the thirst for power, but worst of all, it joined with the growing tide of anti-Semitism. By now this great wave was sweeping all before it; it was useless to try to swim against the current. All who did, men such as John Wycliffe and the English martyrs, were persecuted as heretics. Others, such as the countless Christians who died in the Holocaust, were also swept aside for their opposition to the seed of anti-Semitism firmly embedded in the Christian soul. But soon after the mighty wave climaxed, it suffered an equally dramatic fall and it eventually lapped against the seashore, a spent force. All we are now left with are small pools of water dotted about the sand. We can imagine these pools being full of the purest water (which is where the analogy breaks down, as in reality we'd find sand, oil and assorted debris), representing once again the purest form of the faith, stripped of all the flotsam and jetsam of other cultures and, dare I say, rediscovering its Jewish origins and identity.

The Jews are back in town! The Jews are back in town! These are not the words of a medieval town crier announcing the arrival of the despised Christ killers, but rather the clarion call of history turning full circle. Jews everywhere are rediscovering the faith of their ancestors (though a revival, as such, has not yet arrived), there is a great hunger for true meaning amongst God's chosen people. There is equally a new hunger among many Christians to return to their Jewish roots. I'm not saying that suddenly it's become fashionable to be Jewish and that Gentiles are mysteriously discovering Jewish ancestors, perhaps finding a great-grandfather who lopped a -stein or -berg from the end of their name. What I'm saying is that they are actually discovering the Jewishness of the Bible and the fact that the early Christians, including Jesus, were all Jewish! There are Christians about, believe me, who still don't realise that Jesus and his disciples were as Jewish as Woody Allen or the Marx Brothers; instead they have reinvented him as a faux Gentile.

If you go to any Messianic fellowship these days you'll find as many Gentiles as Jews, usually more. More and more are waking up to the need to bring back the Jewishness of the original Christians, to start to read the Bible with Jewish eyes. Many (I hope) will be reading this book, which is proof in itself, as you wouldn't have got so far if an interest hasn't been kindled. If you are a Christian and wonder where you can go next in response to what you have read in this book, have a look at the Appendices. There you will find a reading list, and information about ministries working for Israel and the Jewish people. Thanks to Fred Wright, there is also a suggested order of service that can be followed by churches and fellowships wishing to make amends for the tragic history of the Jewish people in the Christian world.

Appendix A: Recommended Reading

Cohn-Sherbok, Dan, *The Crucified Jew*, HarperCollins, 1992

Dimont, Max I., *Jews, God and History*, Penguin, 1994

Fisher, Julia, *Israel: The Mystery of Peace*, Authentic, 2003

Gilbert, Martin, *The Atlas of Jewish History*, William Morrow & Co., 1993

Maltz, Steve, *The Land of Many Names*, Authentic, 2003

Richards, Rob, *Has God Finished with Israel?* Word Publishing, 2000

Wilson, Marvin R., *Our Father Abraham*, Eerdmans, 1989

Wright, Fred, *Father, Forgive Us*, Monarch, 2001

Appendix B: Organisations Working for Israel and the Jewish People

This is not an exhaustive list but simply an alphabetic list of ministries that I know of or have come into contact with personally. A fuller list is provided on the website www.thepeopleofmanynames.com

AMITI www.amiti.co.il is a group of Israeli believers visiting churches and fellowships in the UK with teaching, worship, creative arts and dance.

Bridges for Peace www.bridgesforpeace.com is a Jerusalem-based Christian organisation supporting Israel and building relationships between Christians and Jews worldwide through education and practical deeds.

Chesed (email beitsifre@yahoo.co.uk) is committed to bringing comfort to Jews in the former Soviet Union, especially to those who are marginalised.

Christian Witness to Israel www.cwi.org.uk is a UK-based society committed to sharing the Good News of Jesus the Messiah with the Jewish people.

Church's Ministry among Jewish People www.cmj.org. uk is a team of believers, both Jewish and non-Jewish, whose aim is to support and encourage Christians and Jews alike in the area of Messianic faith.

CL Ministries www.clministries.org.uk features Bible teaching from Chris Hill, who also leads Bible tours of Israel, an experience that has greatly enriched Chris's ability to present the Hebrew background to the scriptures in his teaching.

Exobus www.exobus.org provides transport to help bring Jewish people in the former Soviet Union back to Israel.

Focus on Israel www.focus-on-israel.org is committed to God's continuing purposes through fulfilment of the prophetic scriptures.

Jews for Jesus www.jewsforjesus.org.uk exists to make the Messiahship of Jesus an unavoidable issue to Jewish people worldwide.

The Joseph Storehouse www.visionforisrael.com is a charitable organisation established to help rebuild the nation of Israel, both spiritually and physically.

Land & Life www.landandlife.co.uk co-ordinates large and small tours to Israel for Christians.

Light for the Last Days www.lightforthelastdays.co.uk features the teaching ministry of Tony Pearce pointing to the connection between current world events and the Bible prophecies concerning Israel and the Second Coming of Jesus.

Messianic Testimony www.tmtestimony.org.uk is a Christian witness to the Jewish people.

Prayer for Israel (email pfi@btconnect.com) is a network of Christians praying for Israel and the Jewish people worldwide.

Revelation Television www.revelationtv.com is a UK-based Christian satellite TV channel (SKY 676) with a special heart for Israel and the Jewish people.

Appendix C: A Liturgy of Reconciliation

Here is a liturgy adapted, with permission, from Fred Wright's book *Father, Forgive Us*, Appendix I, 'A Liturgy for Yom Ha Shoah'.

The liturgy is a suggested order of service for churches or small groups that want to address the issue of the Christian contributions, and indifference, to Jewish suffering over the last two millennia. It includes a plea for strength and courage to face the problems of Christian anti-Semitism and the bloodstained history of Jewish-Christian relationships. The liturgy concludes with a prayer for reconciliation. Running throughout is the theme of the continuity of Judaism and Christianity. This liturgy would have special significance for *Yom Ha Shoah*, the Jewish day of remembrance of the Holocaust.

Preparation A table should be set with two plain candles. A bowl of water may be included for symbolic hand washing.

Leader Blessed art Thou, O Lord our God, King of the Universe, who has brought us to this time. We light a candle of Remembrance for all those who died as victims of hatred without cause. Let us take a moment to remember them.

One or two minutes with a quiet musical background – preferably a Jewish lament.

Leader We are gathered together in memory of those Jews who have died at the hands of others, particularly as a result of the 'Final Solution of the Jewish Problem' under the tyranny of Nazi Germany. At the same time we remember all those Jewish people, men, women and children, who suffered and died at the hands of Christians as a result of hatred without cause. We pray that the Holy One of Israel in His infinite mercy will grant us a place of intercession for the church, that the hatred without cause will end, that there will be reconciliation between Jew and Gentile and that the church will abandon replacement theology and relate in a biblical manner to the State of Israel.

Let us a take a moment to come before the Lord and confess our personal sins, that we might enter the Holy Place with clean hands and a pure heart. Are we in right relationship with God, our spouses, our children, each other and the church we belong to? *(At this stage a washing of hands may be appropriate as an expression of clean hands and a pure heart.)*

To express our solidarity with the Jewish people we will sing the Shema:

Shema Israel Adoni Eloheynu Adoni echad

Baruch Shem kavod malchuto le olam Va-ed

Leader Why is this night not like other nights?

Congregation Because this night we confess the sin of the church against the Jewish people, we remember their sufferings and declare our intent that the Holocaust and its kind, past and present, will not happen again.

Congregation We confess the sin of anti-Semitism in the church from its early days. We reject all anti-Semitic teaching, all anti-Jewish sentiments, the misreading of scripture, depriving Jesus of his Jewishness, and any theology in which the Jewish people are abandoned by God and replaced by the church. We confess that Christ loved the church and gave his life for those who would be part of it, both Jew and Gentile. We have failed to make Israel jealous, and in our history many times the cross of reconciliation has become a sword of destruction. Lord, have mercy upon us according to your unfailing love. Amen.

Leader Let us confess our position concerning the Jewish people.

Congregation We proclaim that they have not been rejected, that they have not fallen beyond recovery. Theirs remains the adoption as sons, theirs the divine glory, the covenants, the receiving of the law, the Temple worship and the promises. Theirs are the Patriarchs, and from them is traced the human ancestry of Christ, who is God over all, forever praised. Amen.

Leader Praise the Lord.

Congregation The Lord's Great Name be praised forever and to eternity. May the high praises of God be in our hearts and our mouths and may both we and the house of Israel exalt His name together.

Leader Magnified and sanctified be His great name in the world that He has created. According to His will may He establish His kingdom during our life and our days and during the life and the days of the house of Israel. May there be *shalom* both upon us and upon the House of Israel.

Congregation May there be abundant peace from heaven and wellsprings of life. May He who makes peace on the high places make unto us *shalom* and *shalom* to the House of Israel. Amen.

Worship *A song of peace.*

Leader We appeal to you, O Lord Most High, to restore the testimony of the church to the Jewish people.

Congregation O good and merciful Father, what can we say, what can we speak, before your face of righteousness and justice? Our needs are many and our wisdom is slender, but our hope is in you. Restore, O Lord, the honour of your Name and that of your son Yeshua (Jesus), the Messiah of Israel, in the testimony of your church. Shame covers us as often as the remembrance of the teaching of Yeshua and your unending love confronts us. No longer let the Name of Yeshua bring reproach, but let it be received with joy by your people. Amen.

Leader We acknowledge before your throne of mercy, O Lord, the sin of indifference and ambivalence.

Congregation Forbid it, Lord, that, as in times past and particularly in the Holocaust, we should stand idly by crowned with indifference as your people suffer. Give us a courageous spirit to stand up against all injustice and anti-

Semitic positions. Forgive all silence where there should have been speech; forgive us for abandoning your children to the flames.

Leader May your loving-kindness and mercy not depart from us. Create in us a heart of love for your people and deliver us from all future reproach.

Congregation Blessed is the man that walks not in the counsel of the wicked nor stands in the ways of sinners nor sits in the seat of scoffers. Let our delight be in you, O Lord, and your word.

Leader We give thanks that your word is a lamp to our feet and a light unto our path and we walk in darkness at our peril. Lord, let us be good and faithful hearers and teachers of your word.

Congregation Lord, we acknowledge that your word is our fence and our safety. Let us walk in the light of your word and live our lives accordingly. We believe that as faithful students of your word we will be equipped to deal with anti-Semitism in the church and the world at large.

Worship *A song of reconciliation.*

Leader We now turn to specifics and we will respond by repudiating and renouncing the causes of anti-Semitism and recognising the activities of sin. Inasmuch as it depends upon us we will ensure that such things never happen again.

Leader For the anti-Semitism of the early church fathers, the demonisation of the Jews and the charge of 'Christ killers'.

Congregation We reject and renounce this teaching in Jesus' name.

Leader As for the teaching of contempt.

Congregation We renounce all blood libels, charges of profaning the host and conspiracy theories in Jesus' name.

Leader As for the demonisation of the Jews.

Congregation We renounce and acknowledge as sin the demonisation of Jewish people. We renounce all negative stereotypes in Jesus' name. We confess that the Jewish people remain your beloved.

Leader As for the Crusades.

Congregation We acknowledge that the Crusades brought a dark stain to the history of the church, when the cross was turned into a sword. We renounce the Crusaders' activities as an expression of Christ and his Kingdom. As for all movements that persecuted and destroyed your people in the name of Jesus and his church, we acknowledge these as sin.

Leader As for the Office of the Inquisition.

Congregation We acknowledge the persecution of Jews and *Marranos* as sin and renounce the practices of this office and its inheritance in Jesus' name.

Leader As for the anti-Semitism of the Reformation.

Congregation We renounce and reject the anti-Semitism of the Reformation and its ongoing effects.

Leader As for the failure of the church to respond to Nazism and Fascism and for its collaboration in some areas.

Congregation We renounce cowardice and failure to respond to such challenges in Jesus' name.

Leader As for Replacement Theology.

Congregation We renounce and reject Replacement Theology as teaching contrary to your word and your purposes. We confess that the Jewish people are not redundant, cast aside, forgotten or without hope or purpose. We believe that they have a hope and a future.

Leader We recall the words that remembrance leads to deliverance, whilst forgetfulness leads to destruction.

Congregation We proclaim before heaven, which is your throne, and earth, which is your footstool, that inasmuch as it depends upon us we will combat anti-Semitism in all its forms. We will remember those who have died because of hatred without cause. We pray that, by our endeavours, their flame might not be extinguished, their names that were consigned to ashes and dust will be remembered and be a blessing for the future and their deaths might not be meaningless.

Leader As we have approached your throne of grace and mercy, we boldly request, O Lord our Father, that you will use us to correct the anti-Semitic ills of the past and use us as instruments of your grace and mercy from this time forth.

Worship *A song of strengthening.*

Conclusion

Leader We have gathered together today in the presence of Almighty God to state our purpose and intent to depart from the anti-Semitic inheritance of the church. It is an awesome thing to be in the presence of the living God. We will now light a candle of Hope from the candle of Remembrance and ask that the symbol of the two candles might remind us of the transaction that has taken place here today.

Aaronic Blessing

(Hebrew read by Leader and English by Congregation)

Y'varekh'kha Adonai v'yishmerekha
[May the Lord bless you and keep you]

Ya'er Adonai panav eleikha vichunekka
[The Lord make His face shine upon you and show you His favour]

Yissa Adonai panav eleikha v'yasem l'kha shalom
[May the Lord lift up His face toward you and give you peace]

The Lord's *shalom* be upon you, your house and those you love, and upon the House of Israel. Amen.

The Land of Many Names
Steve Maltz

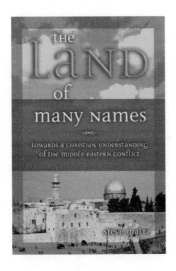

Much heat has been generated by the subject of Israel and Palestine. It's a subject that will not go away and it is crucial that Christians should have a clear grasp of both the spiritual and historical issues involved.

This is a lively, entertaining and provocative introduction to the subject for ordinary Christians. The author takes you on a historical journey of the *Land of Many Names*, from the Canaan of Abraham to the Promised Land, by way of the Land of Milk and Honey, Israel and Judah, Judea and Samaria, Palestine, The Holy Land, Zion, Israel and 'The Zionist Entity'. At each stage, we pause to consider what God is saying to all concerned and, in some places, awkward questions are also asked of the reader.

This is an easy read, but it is not a comfortable book.

Has God Finished with Israel?
Rob Richards

Much has been written and said by Christians on the whole issue of Israel, much of it triumphant, insensitive and simplistic. This book stems the flow. It is the journey of one man challenged, by God, to take a close look at the place of Israel within the purposes of God.

In this book, Rob Richards seeks to discover the answer to probing questions such as:

- Are Jewish people still the 'chosen people' and if so, for what?
- What does the Bible have to say about the covenants and the promised Messiah?
- How do events in Israel today fit in with biblical prophecy?

Israel: The Mystery of Peace
Julia Fisher

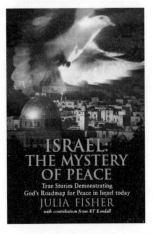

Israel: The Mystery of Peace contains incredible up-to-date true stories of hope and reconciliation from the Middle East that, remarkably, are holding firm despite the ongoing unrest in Israel today. These stories, researched in depth by Julia Fisher, demonstrate that there is another road map for peace emerging in Israel today – God's road map – where, despite politics and war, Jews, Arabs and Christians are praying and working together demonstrating that genuine peace is possible.

Read about . . .

. . . **Jonathan Miles** who arranges for Palestinian Children from Gaza to have life-saving operations in Israel.

. . . **a nun from France** who walked across Europe to Jerusalem where she met a former Orthodox Jew, a German Protestant and an Arab Christian from the Old City . . . read how God has brought their paths together.

. . . **a couple from New York** who run an addiction centre for Arabs and Jews in northern Israel.

. . . **a man born** into a Muslim family in Algeria, who escaped from a terrorist training camp and is now living in Jerusalem, actively involved in reconciliation between Arabs and Jews.

. . . **RT Kendall**, the former minister of Westminster Chapel, who shares his experience of meeting and praying for Yasser Arafat.

For release in 2006. . .

The Man of Many Names
Steve Maltz

A look at Jesus Christ through Jewish eyes.

- Who were they expecting?
- Why did they reject him?
- What do they think of him now?

Insights into the prophecies of, the person and the mission of the Messiah.